The
RACE

Marked Out for Us

How to Catch Your Breath, Set Your Eyes,
and Find Your Footing in Biblical Faith

FOREWORD BY SANDRA STANLEY

DOT BOWEN

THE RACE MARKED OUT FOR US

Dedications

To Brenda Tuminello, for teaching me how to hold on to the faith while God held on to you after the loss of your child and through your battle with breast cancer. Your countenance displayed the presence and power of God. I told you I wanted to dedicate this book to you just three days before you entered into eternity with God. It is finally completed, and I want to say thank you for the inspiration you were to me. I know Jesus stood and applauded you as you entered into His presence.

To Janice, my dear sister. I have never seen anyone grasp the hand of Jesus like you. Through such pain and heartache, you turn each hurt and each tear into worship of our Savior. I thank God for giving me a front-row seat to see you follow Jesus without counting the cost. You are my hero, and I love you more than you will ever know.

Contents

Foreword

Life is a journey. We hear that a lot. There are sunny days, and ones where the rain relentlessly pours. There are seasons of joy, and times when it's hard to find anything to be joyful about. Through all of the ups and downs, and all of the different chapters and seasons, God is weaving and working and building something beautiful.

One of my all-time favorite verses of Scripture falls right smack in the middle of a pretty famous psalm of David's. Psalm 139 speaks of God's extraordinary awareness of you. He sees you. He knows you. And there is never any point in trying to hide from His sight. From there David continues by highlighting God's intimate involvement in knitting you together and creating you uniquely and wonderfully. But here's my favorite part: "All the days ordained for me were written in your book before one of them came to be" (verse 16, NIV). Not only did He make you, He knows every single one of your days, and He's known them always. How cool is that?

Fast-forward to the New Testament. The writer of the book of Hebrews uses the metaphor of a race: "let us run with perseverance the race marked out for us" (Hebrews 12:1, NIV). God has a plan, a race, for you.

I am so excited about The Race Marked Out for Us by Dot Bowen. I've known Dot for over thirty years, and I've watched much of her journey unfold. I've had the privilege of a front-row seat, and I've seen her devotion to God and to her family. I've also watched her heart break over women who are far from God. I've heard her prayers and I've seen her tears as ladies have shared their stories with her. Over the past couple years, I've seen great clarity come as she's sharpened her focus and refined her ministry vision to do whatever it takes to help women successfully run their races.

In The Race Marked Out for Us, Dot harnesses her harrowing story of running a half marathon without proper preparation. In doing so, she draws life-changing parallels between her own race experience and running the race God has laid out for each of us. As you dive into the book, you'll be confronted with ten essential lessons that will propel you forward in your race. I believe these ten things will lead you in a journey to freedom, contentment, peace, and the ability to finish strong.

As you're about to discover, Dot's humor, combined with her deep knowledge and love of Scripture, lays an amazing foundation that will embolden your own journey to run the race God has for you—the one He's known about from the beginning of time.

— **Sandra Stanley**

Introduction

*Therefore, since we are surrounded
by such a great cloud of witnesses, let
us throw off everything that hinders
and the sin that so easily entangles.
And let us run with perseverance
the race marked out for us.*

HEBREWS 12:1 & 2, NIV

Looking out the window with tears streaming down my face, I cried out, "God, what is happening to me?"

I knew something was going on inside of my mind and body, but I didn't know what. One day I would be happy, and the next day I would find myself crying without reason. I remember my husband, Howard, saying to me, "In over 25 years of marriage, you have never acted like this! What is going on with you?" I would have loved to give him an answer. Howard so wanted to "fix" me, but how can you fix something when you don't even know what's broken?

One afternoon in the middle of all the madness, I felt like I had to get out of the house or I would scream. So I decided to take a walk. Fifteen minutes in, I realized that I no longer wanted to run away from home, and I had stopped crying! Had walking miraculously affected my emotions? I have always hated exercise and, to be honest, I still do. But I was desperate. You can rest assured that if I was considering walking, other than through a mall, I was desperate! My sweet family had no idea what to do or say to their mother. Howard never knew who he would get when he got home. I knew something needed to change.

At this point you may be able to guess that I was in the beginning stages of menopause, and whenever I started to walk, the endorphins would kick in and help my lack of hormones. Because I was desperate, and exercise seemed to help a little, I decided the thing to do was to join a gym. Now, in complete transparency, I cannot count how many gyms I have joined over my lifetime. I can, however, tell you that joining a gym doesn't make you lose weight or create a desire to exercise. That requires actually going to the gym. And even though going didn't make me enjoy it—not even once—I figured that if exercise helped me not hurt my family, then exercise it must be!

So why would someone who hates to exercise, walk, or run, write a book titled *The Race Marked Out for Us?* I remember asking God this very question. One day in my prayer time, I told God I did not feel confident writing or teaching anything about running because I am not a runner. His voice was not audible, but I felt as if I could literally hear God talk to me.

"Oh, you are a runner all right! You have been running all your life, looking and longing for something to make you happy. You have tried to find yourself by running to things you feel will bring you value, things that consume your time, and activities that make you feel important."

As much as it stung, I knew it was true. I am a runner. If there's one thing I have done consistently in my life, it's running. I don't mean 5K races or half marathons. I have been running to things I think will make me happy, or from things that don't make me happy. I have run from God, and I have run to Him. I have run to other people to find acceptance, and I've run to vanity and material possessions in an effort to fill an emptiness that could not be filled with any of those things. Yes, I would say when it comes to running, I am a professional. Running from God almost cost me the life I longed for and robbed me of the desires of my heart.

I may not know you personally, but I have talked with many women who are deciding whether to run to God so He can give them the life they long for, or to run to other people, places, or things that have no ability to fulfill the desires of their heart.

I believe you, too, are a runner, and I have some great news for all of us runners in the chapters ahead. I will tell you the story of how I entered Disney's half marathon and the lessons I learned as I ran. But I will also share with you what I realized as I was writing: these were the same lessons God had been teaching me in the race of life. Yes, as followers of Jesus we have been set in a race called life, and we run with Him, for Him, and because of Him.

So, get ready to journey with me as I share with you the day I was running for my life. I pray that reading my story might create in you a heart to run for your own life. One thing is for sure: I believe the truths in this book will give you a desire to run your own race in such a way that you will win!

Together, we can learn how to run for our lives and, in return, find the life God has created us to live.

Are you ready?

Let's run!

— Dot

You Had Me at Hello

*And we know that for those who
love God all things work together
for good, for those who are called
according to his purpose.*

Romans 8:28

I t only took one phone call to change the direction of my life.

The call that changed my life didn't come in the middle of the night, nor did it have a message of bad news attached to it. My call came in the middle of the day. Right after I said hello, I heard my oldest daughter, Christy, say, "Hey, Mom, I've been looking online and noticed Disney is having a half marathon. I think we should sign up and run." I asked her if she thought she had called someone else, because obviously this invitation was not meant for me. It's no secret to Christy—or anyone else, for that matter—that I do not exercise. I hate running, I hate sweating, I did not know what a half marathon actually was, and I told her all those things. She laughed and said, "I know, Mom, but you have an entire year to train, and after we run the race we can enjoy the park with the kids. It will be a family vacation!"

Vacation?! Now, *that's* what I'm talking about! Christy knew if she mentioned "vacation" and "grandkids," she would have me at hello. And she did! I said yes and signed up online immediately. I was so excited to be able to go to Disney and spend a few days with the grandkids at their favorite place on earth. From then on, every time we were around the grandchildren, Howard and I found it difficult to talk about anything other than our trip to Disney. Howard, that sweet husband of mine, made reservations for all of us to stay at the Grand Floridian, Disney's most elegant resort. This place has its own spa, beaches, and a stop on the monorail, making it possible to get to all the different resorts and parks without ever having to get into your car. I could not wait for this family vacation! All I had to do was get the half marathon out of the way, and then I could spend the rest of the time enjoying the spa, the different parks, and watching my kids and grandkids ride their favorite rides.

With the family vacation in mind, it never occurred to me that maybe I should research how to train for and run a half marathon, especially since I had no clue what I signed up for. Christy's excitement on the phone was contagious, but I did not have time to learn about running or training. I did what I needed to do at the moment, which was to get off the phone and sign up. It's amazing what my kids or grandkids can talk me into!

The call came at a time in my life when I really needed a vacation. I had just founded a new women's ministry, Cup of Joy, and I was overwhelmed. God had placed a burden on my heart for "the lady who tried to be everything to everybody"—the woman who would one day realize she couldn't measure up to the expectations she placed on herself or the expectations she felt from others, and who would then withdraw and give up trying to please anyone, including God. One of the many reasons I felt the need to rescue this woman from the lies she believed is because *I was this woman.* I tried so hard to be what everyone expected me to be that I eventually lost my true identity.

Gradually, God opened my eyes to the truth: He created me to be me, and if I spent my life bending and becoming someone else in an effort to please others, I might as well attempt to walk on water or hold on to the wind. It is impossible! Even so, it took years of renewing my mind with God's truth before I could embrace the real me, and even now I sometimes have to remind myself that I'm loved and accepted by God.

There are still many days I don't feel worthy of love or acceptance, but it's not about feeling worthy; it's about embracing His love even when we feel unlovable.

My ministry was founded on this truth that had clearly transformed my life, but that was really the only thing I knew. I certainly didn't know how to run a ministry! I had no idea how much time, money, and faith it would take. God used my lack of experience as one more tool to bring me face-to-face with the truth that my worth and purpose come from Him, not in my ability to successfully run a ministry. I had to cling to the truth that He called me into this ministry, and He would teach me how to trust Him to lead Cup of Joy.

In that busy season, the last thing I was thinking about was training for my half marathon. Every thought and spare bit of energy I had was spent trying to be faithful to God's calling to teach and equip women to run their own spiritual race. Though I wasn't training for the race, my mind often turned to the trip to Disney on the days I felt overwhelmed and discouraged—I would just think about our family vacation and get fresh excitement and energy. I'd smile at the thought of finishing the race and then taking a few days to enjoy the family, relax in the spa at the hotel, and watch the kids have their full Disney experience.

Whenever I tell my half marathon story, no one, especially true runners, can comprehend that I would even think about running in a half marathon without training. No one does that! But it just wasn't on my radar. The only time I even thought about the race was when I received an e-mail from Disney asking how my training was going. I would think, *"What training?"* I know now how ridiculous this all sounds, signing up for a half marathon without even knowing how many miles a half marathon is or what to expect!

In reflecting on all the things I should have known but did not, I am reminded of my friend Allison and her beautiful daughter, Alina. Allison and her husband, Rob, conquered many hurdles to adopt Alina from Ukraine. It took some time for Alina to find her stride in her new home, but it all seemed to click when she joined her neighborhood swim team.

If you have ever been to a neighborhood swim meet, you know what a big deal they are. In order to organize a neighborhood swim meet you need to recruit swimmers, create legal documents for liability, buy lane ropes, get banners, pay coaches, find pennant flags, plug in a sound system, beg volunteers, pay judges, and recruit computer workers. It's not a simple event. The day of the meet looks like an Olympic event. Each swimmer is given a number, which is then written on their arms to remind them which events they're competing in. Once their age group and numbers are called, the kids line up to jump in the pool and race. When things get going, it's hard to even carry on a conversation surrounded by parents cheering and shouting instructions to their children.

Allison told me a story about one particular race that took place after Alina had been on the neighborhood swim team for three years. It was the last swim meet of the summer, and as Allison wrote Alina's race number on her arm, she said, "Alina, swim fast and win your last race!" Allison had barely gotten the words out when Alina looked at her with her beautiful brown eyes drawn wide and asked in surprise, "Is this a race?!" Allison was caught off guard. *Did she just ask if this was a race?!*

You see, Alina never considered her swim meets as races. All three years that she swam on the team, when the whistle blew, Alina would jump in the pool with a huge smile on her face and just swim, enjoying every moment. It never occurred to her that she was in a competition and needed to outpace the other swimmers. In other words, she was in a world—or should I say pool—of her own, enjoying the water and the cheers of her family and friends.

When Allison told me this story, I could not stop laughing! But then it hit me: I had also entered into a race and had no idea what to do. Until that very moment, the race had been nothing more than just a means to an end. And trust me when I say that it just about brought me to my end. More on that later.

I wish I could say this was the only race I entered where I did not know what I was doing, but unfortunately, it's not.

The other race I entered also started with a call. This race is the one Jesus called me to when I heard Him say, "Follow Me." And, much like saying yes to a half marathon without knowing what it was, the day I heard Jesus' call to follow Him, I had no clue what I was doing. He just had me at hello! At that moment when I placed my trust in Jesus, God entered my name into this race called the Christian life and mapped out for me the path He would ask me to run with Him. I was in no way prepared to run this race God had set for me.

If you have made a commitment to follow Jesus, did you know that it is God who establishes your steps as you journey through this race called life? Our life with Jesus starts with a call, and our spiritual journey begins the minute we accept it. Paul writes to the church in Rome, "Do you not know that in a race all the runners run, but only one receives the prize? So run that you may obtain it." (1 Corinthians 9:24)

I want to be honest with you. Not only did I not know I was in a race (much less that I was a runner!), I was *definitely* not winning. For years after I gave my life to Jesus, I didn't understand what it meant to be a follower of Christ. I did not understand the Bible, nor did I understand how to know God. I couldn't comprehend how I could have a personal relationship with my Creator. As far as my spiritual life was concerned, I felt like I was in the deep end of the pool, sinking down after trying to stay afloat, and no one was paying attention.

There were good days that gave me a little hope, but even then, I never felt like I accomplished much or that God was very happy I was on His team. I tried very hard to be a better Christian, but despite all my efforts, I still felt stuck. It didn't matter how hard I tried, It seemed like as soon as I made a little progress, something would happen and knock me back farther than I had ever moved forward.

I was overwhelmed with the responsibilities of living like a Christian, and I felt defeated most of the time. To be quite honest, there were days when drowning seemed to be the best option. I never once felt God was pleased with my performance, and since we're laying all the cards on the table here, I wasn't very pleased with His, either!

When Christy called me about the race, I remember saying, "Do you know who I am? I am NOT a runner!" In a similar way, when Jesus asked me to run with Him, I remember praying and asking Him, "Do you know who I am? I am a sinner!" I felt in my heart that I could hear Him say, "Yes, I know. And it's good you know, too, so you can also know I am your Savior."

My parents never pushed us to go to church, and they themselves never went, but if I wanted to go they would drop me off and pick me up after the service. It was easier to go with my aunt, who was very active in her small Baptist church in Chattanooga, Tennessee. The church was so small that it was obvious when a guest was visiting. I especially stood out because not only was I a visitor, I was also the youngest person in the building. I'm not being extreme when I say I might have been the only person who was breathing without an oxygen tank! They were precious people, but the only thing we had in common was that we all were trying to make it through the day alive.

I will never forget how scared I was when the preacher would really get into his sermon and start running up and down the aisles of the church. He'd start at a normal tone and then ramp up the volume and speed until he was yelling and trying to catch his breath between words. It seemed like he would look straight at me and say, "If you don't have Jesus, you will go to hell!" I guess he was trying to scare the hell out of me, which was effective, because I was *very* scared of hell. I didn't have a clue what hell was, but it didn't sound like a great place to visit—and certainly no place to spend eternity. When the preacher asked if anyone wanted to escape hell, I never moved so fast in my life! I felt like I had wings as I ran down to the front of the church. I'm sure the look on my face was sheer fright as I shouted, "I want Jesus! I do not want to go to hell!"

The pastor prayed with me and I asked Jesus to forgive me. Because of His promise of forgiveness, I had become His child and He became my heavenly Father. I could talk with Him whenever I wanted, and we didn't have to just talk about hell. I remember tears streaming down my face as, for the first time, I felt loved and accepted unconditionally.

———————

Unfortunately, feelings come and go.

I enjoyed the peace of forgiveness for about a week. I don't know exactly how long I was able to live as God wanted me to, but I know it wasn't very long. I honestly had no idea what my salvation meant, other than I was a forgiven child going to heaven and not hell. My life, my actions, my insecurities, and my desires didn't change very much. I could never feel forgiven, no matter how many times I was told I was. Every time I went to church, I "rededicated" my life, which kept me satisfied for a while until I felt like a sinner again.

It was only when I began to truly study the Scriptures that I found the assurance of my salvation. If I couldn't save myself, I surely couldn't keep myself saved. This truth alone gave me a greater appreciation of grace, love, and acceptance. Obviously, we all sin, and the Bible does say we must repent and ask for forgiveness, but I wasn't as concerned about sin as I was afraid of Jesus leaving me and being sentenced to hell.

One area the enemy constantly attacked me was by making me feel like I would never be good enough to be loved and accepted by anyone. I knew my earthly dad and mom loved me, but they had a difficult time expressing it. They both lost their parents early and had to survive on their own. They didn't have parents to tell them how much they loved them, so they didn't understand how much I needed to hear the words "I love you." In fact, I never actually heard those words come out of my dad's mouth until he was dying.

Over the years, my mom started to tell me she loved me after I made an intentional decision to say it first. It lasted that way for some time, until eventually she took the lead. I never experienced this with my dad, but I knew and felt his love for me in the way he served our family. It just wasn't enough for me sometimes. As you can imagine, a young teenager looking for love in all the wrong places and wanting to feel accepted was a disaster waiting to happen. I shudder to think what I would have done if I lived in today's world with almost anything imaginable right at our fingertips. Though I didn't live in a world where everything is accepted and accessible, I still tried to gain acceptance from boys. I lived almost my entire life never feeling loved and accepted unconditionally until I met my husband Howard—God's gracious gift to me.

As much as I enjoy and appreciate experiencing Howard's love and acceptance, when life gets hard, it is only God's love and acceptance that brings hope. God has taught me through my mistakes and even the deceptions of Satan that I have always been loved and accepted by Him. In some ways, my inability to feel my dad's love (even though he loved me) is the same lie I believed about God. I thought God couldn't love me because of the things I had done, but He does! I wish I had been able to be satisfied with God's love rather than trying to find it in boyfriends, but as a teenager I wanted something tangible, someone I could touch and see.

Why do we long to hear someone else say they love us rather than the very One who gave His life in the greatest act of love the world has ever known?

I know I struggle w/ this, as a single person

I think the answer is found in one word: *Feelings*. When my circumstances got hard to manage, I continually felt as if God had walked away from me. The truth of the matter is that I was the one who walked away from God emotionally, until eventually I ran from Him. I was a young adult when I started to run from God, and before I knew it I became an experienced runner. It was only when I found myself so exhausted from running toward everything that did not satisfy that I finally surrendered with a broken heart. After so much running and being in such a state of exhaustion and despair, I decided I wanted nothing to do with Jesus . . . and yet I couldn't let Him go.

At my darkest point, I hated my life. I felt like I didn't love Howard anymore, but felt trapped without a choice to leave. We had young children and, even though I was so miserable, I did enjoy being a mom. I decided to go speak with my sister's pastor. I'll never forget what he said to me: "Doris, do you ever want to look back and wonder what God would have done if you had trusted and obeyed Him?" Even though I hadn't listened to Him in ages, I sensed the Spirit telling me that I needed to obey God at all costs. I will never forget sitting on the sofa one Sunday morning, torn between wanting to run and wanting to be found by God. I just wanted to be happy again. I wanted my marriage to be healed and to rediscover a love for Howard I knew only God could give me. I started lapping through the Bible that was next to me, and I stopped at John 6:66-69:

> *After this many of his disciples turned back and no longer walked with him. So Jesus said to the twelve, "Do you want to go away as well?" Simon Peter answered him, "Lord, to whom shall we go? You have the words of eternal life, and we have*

believed, and have come to know, that you are
the Holy One of God."
John 6:66-69

I knew I had read this conversation between Jesus and His disciples before, but this time the words pierced my heart. Jesus knew that at that moment, I wanted to walk away from the God I had come to know, and He was asking me, "Are you running again?" I sat there and cried like a baby, thinking, "Where can I go and to whom can I run? Everywhere I had been and everything I had run to only left me emptier. I know now that God was leading me to Him. Minutes after reading these verses, a preacher named Dr. Charles Stanley came on the television and began to preach on forgiveness. I don't remember much of the sermon other than the powerful words, "You are forgiven." I don't know how I got from the sofa to my knees, but with tears running down my face and my heart breaking in two, I found myself in front of the TV crying and asking, "Is this true . . . am I forgiven?"

This time, forgiveness was sweeter than before. I did not want to be forgiven to avoid hell; I wanted forgiveness to have Jesus. From that moment until today, I have continued to feel His love. His presence. His power, and yes. His forgiveness! I have often joked with Him, saying "Jesus, Velcro yourself to me! You may not let go of me, but I might let go of you!" Neither one of us has let go since that Sunday morning. The words "you are forgiven" changed my life forever. I never want to live in condemnation for all I have done, but I also never want to forget what God has done in my life. His grace and love is greater than my pain and my sin. Jesus called me to follow Him, and this time I gathered all the broken pieces of my life and handed my heart to Him. I can almost hear His words even after all these years. "Come and enter into my rest. I will give you rest from seeking the love and approval of others because you have always had My love and approval . . . and I am all you need."

I won't say our life together has *always* been easy, but it has been satisfying and purposeful. Running with Jesus has its ups and downs, but it has never been like it was in those former years. I think the difference is brokenness. I was so broken that I knew I needed Him and, more importantly, I *wanted* Him. Jesus and I have traveled many different paths together. I still struggle to trust God when my emotions are working overtime, but overall nothing has been sweeter than the moments when I feel His loving arms around me, drawing me to His heart. When I face my anxiety, I'm reminded that God has promised to never leave me. I'm never alone or abandoned; I have Him and He has me!

Yes, it's true, I have been called by God to run the race He has set for me, and I can run without getting tired or growing weary because He has given me His power to run.

I have found hope and encouragement in knowing that I am His child, His beloved, and He is my Father. My sweet Savior is a loving, forgiving, and good Father.

The best part of my life started with "The Call" to follow Him, and the greatest moment in this race will be the day He calls me home. The blood of Jesus paid my entrance fee into the presence of God forever. All I had to do was say yes when He called me to follow Him. Every morning of this race, with every new mercy, Jesus has me at "hello!"

Father, I thank You I can call You Father. What a privilege to be called Your child through the blood of Jesus Christ. Thank You for the gift of forgiveness, mercy, and grace as I run the race You have set for me. I had no idea when I accepted Your call to follow You that You entered me into the Christian race to run with You, for You, and because of You. May I run for Your glory only! I love You Jesus! You are mine and I am Yours.

The Training Program

*For the moment all discipline
seems painful rather than pleasant,
but later it yields the peaceful
fruit of righteousness to those
who have been trained by it.*

HEBREWS 12:11

There's nothing like a half marathon to highlight the struggle between the urgent and the important.

In my mind, a year for training seemed like WAY TOO LONG, especially to spend it doing something I hated, like exercise. Every morning I made my to-do list, and every night I moved what didn't get done to tomorrow's list. At this point I was in way over my head trying to lead a women's ministry. Between teaching, writing, planning, and meeting with women who were struggling in their relationships with Jesus, I barely had the energy to eat dinner. I get why Sarah laughed at God when He said she would have a child in her old age; some things are best done when we are young.

I kept receiving monthly training e-mails from Disney, and every single time they popped up I thought, *I really need to start this training.* Then I closed my computer and immediately forgot Disney and training altogether. First, they were monthly e-mails. Then they started coming in more often. I was so impressed with the thoughtfulness and concern Disney World appeared to have for me and my training. Although I appreciated their care, all of my concern was directed toward my nonprofit ministry (emphasis on the "nonprofit"), my husband, my family, and trying to maintain friendships along the way. I had no margin to add training for a race to my busy schedule. Besides, I've known how to run since childhood. How hard could a half marathon be?

My perspective changed the day I got my Disney e-mail saying they were so excited to see me that week. I immediately called Christy and said, "Do you realize we leave for the half marathon this week?!" She said, "Of course, did you forget?" No, I didn't forget. I just didn't realize the year had passed as quickly as it did. Where did the time go? What about training?! It was obviously too late to think about that; now it was time to run.

As I reflect back on this time, I still can't believe I actually thought I could complete a half marathon without training, but that's exactly how I lived every single day leading up to the race. Looking back over my life, it's so easy to see a pattern in this way of thinking. Whatever my parents tried to teach me, I always thought I knew more than they did. I manipulated things so that everything worked out just the way I wanted. Of course, the older I got, the harder it was to control my circumstances. What I thought I had control over suddenly controlled me. Believing I could control outcomes and circumstances is as foolish as believing I could run a half marathon without training . . . and I believed both these things!

All Scripture is breathed out by God and profitable for teaching, for reproof, for correction, and for training in righteousness,
2 TIMOTHY 3:16

It's true that my spiritual life (or race) started the day I decided to follow Jesus. God opened my eyes to the truth that His Son Jesus had died for my sins, and I only needed to accept His payment and receive forgiveness to become His child. What a wonderful truth! I learned this when I heard the preacher teach from the book of John, and God's Word pressed into my heart with undeniable peace. I was forgiven. I was His child. The next step was learning how to follow Jesus as God's forgiven child. Unfortunately, Jesus did not send me monthly e-mails asking how my training was going.

I doubt very seriously that I would have paid any more attention to Jesus' e-mails than I did to Disney's. I was never taught the importance of knowing Scripture. I grew up thinking that if you went to church and heard the preacher talk about the Bible, that was all you needed to know until the next week. The problem was, I didn't go back every week. My sporadic Sunday doses of Scripture didn't last long. It wasn't until I had no place left to turn and life became impossible that I thought to open the Bible, and even then, I would usually turn to the book of John and read a few verses about God's love, or a few Psalms, to find some kind of relief for my dysfunctional life. David's cries and complaints to God were a comfort to me. I could understand why he asked God to destroy his enemies. But to be honest, I was looking to the Bible to find excuses for my behavior and lack of faith.

It took many years of studying and reading before I came to this realization:

The Bible is about God's story, not about mine.

I discovered how little I knew about the race God set out for me and how clueless I was about the need for training. I didn't know that proper training could have a huge impact on the outcome of my life.

The apostle Paul uses running a race as a metaphor to encourage the new believers who had put their faith in Jesus. In his letters to the churches in Corinth, Galatia, and Philippi, Paul encourages new believers to run the race God has set for them, and to run it as though they would win. As I have said, when I gave my life to Jesus, I didn't know I had signed up for a race, much less that I should get some training! I had no idea Jesus wanted me to live a life *worthy of my calling* as a child of God. It took years before I realized that God was using difficult circumstances, relationships, physical limitations, and my past regrets, along with many other things, to train me for the call He had placed on my life. I fought against everything that was emotionally and physically difficult in order to make this world—*my world*—happy and fulfilling.

Giving my life to Christ means a lot more than escaping hell. It means I no longer control my life. It isn't mine, but God's. I found out the hard way that it doesn't work to give my life to Christ AND try to keep it for myself. I can't live as if my life is mine from Monday through Saturday, and then on Sunday God can take over for the day. I enjoyed having God when I needed Him or when things were going pretty well. I basically lived the way I wanted...until I could no longer control my circumstances. I thought I was supposed to choose how I wanted to live and just ask God to do what I couldn't. This is why my Christian life felt a lot like a game of tug-of-war. On one side was me, trying to do what I wanted, and on the other side was Christ, leading me in His direction. Trust me when I say, God ALWAYS wins at tug-of-war!

*I have been crucified with Christ. It is no longer I
who live, but Christ who lives in me.*
GALATIANS 2:20

In Paul's letter to the church at Galatia, he reminds the believers that they had been crucified with Christ. The first time I read this I thought, *What in the world does THAT mean?* I had never heard a preacher talk about this before. I was very happy to know Jesus died on the cross for me, but no one told me that I had to die too! I didn't know that God had a plan for my life, and that living surrendered to His will would actually please Him AND me.

Yes, Jesus paid for our sins on the cross and freed us from its penalty, but there is still a daily death we must submit to in order to truly experience this freedom. Salvation is free, but experiencing life in its fullness requires knowing how to live in a new way. Just before Jesus went to the cross, He prayed to the Father that His will would be done, not his own. If we follow Jesus, doesn't it make sense that we should have the same mind-set? My sweet friend, if we are to have the same mind-set as Jesus, we have to surrender our will to the Father's. And this is no easy task.

The metaphor of marriage illustrates our life with Christ. When two people come together as husband and wife, they are two individuals, but their commitment to each other makes them one. In the same way, as a follower of Christ, we do not lose our personality or our created being; instead, we surrender all that personality and created being to the perfect will of the Father. When we accept Christ as our Savior, we are united with Christ as one, and it is Christ who lives His life in us. I can live the life Christ has set for me only through His power living and working in me. No matter how much I desire to live a life that is pleasing to God, in my flesh that's impossible. This is why Jesus told His disciples it was better for them that He went away, because He would send the Holy Spirit to help them. It is the Holy Spirit's job to enable and empower us to do whatever God has asked us to do.

I draw my strength from Him by praying and choosing to trust Jesus to live His life in me.

It's a matter of faith, not ability.

This truth is vital for me, because some of the things God asks of me are outside my abilities. For instance, the ability to forgive is difficult in my human strength. If it was up to me, I would take revenge, not offer forgiveness. But because Jesus has forgiven me, I can forgive. Jesus *always* has the ability and desire to forgive, so I can draw on Him to forgive through me.

I am ashamed of how many years I called myself a follower of Christ when, in my heart, I really just wanted Jesus to follow me. In my mind, Jesus still hung on the cross. Although I celebrated Easter and His resurrection, it never really occurred to me that Jesus is now seated on His throne, the seat of all power and authority. HE is in control, not the other way around. My place is at His feet in worship, not sitting in His throne. The only question is, will I choose it?

It was not until I experienced the consequences of my choices that I began to understand the power of choice. It is a power God has given me, and with this power comes great responsibility.

Never underestimate the power of choice.

God chose to give us freedom of choice, and humanity chose to use that freedom independently of God. The entire human race—indeed, every part of creation—has suffered from the moment Adam and Eve chose to disobey God. Each of us individually chooses to disobey Him as well. The choices I made in my half marathon almost cost me my life, but the choices I made in my Christian race just about cost me the enjoyment and contentment of living my life with Jesus.

My lack of spiritual understanding became apparent when my dad got sick. We knew he was not doing well, but not how sick he really was. My dad was a smoker ever since he was a young boy. Back then no one talked about the dangers of smoking. His mom had died when he was young, and the one person still in his life, his father, was a smoker. I hated that my parents smoked. I didn't want to sit near them while they smoked and could never bring myself to pass the pack of cigarettes when they asked. I watched as lung cancer took both of my parents, so believe me, no one hates smoking more than me. I'm not writing to discuss the dangers of smoking, but it did play a part in God training me as His child.

My dad was coughing a lot, which was nothing unusual for a smoker. What we didn't know was that he had started coughing up blood. It got so bad that he finally had to tell us and we immediately took him to the doctor. The report came back, and it wasn't good: cancer. He started seeing a team of doctors, but never felt comfortable with any doctor he visited in Chattanooga. To my surprise, he agreed to try a doctor in Atlanta at my request. Now I had another problem: I did not know an oncologist in Atlanta. Howard had just taken a new job in Atlanta, so we were still getting our feet under us. Meanwhile, the doctors in Chattanooga were talking about giving my dad chemo and, for the first time in my life, I saw fear in his eyes. I remember walking into his room and seeing him embracing my mom. I heard him say, "Ruby, we have made it through a lot of things, and we will make it through this."

You really have a new appreciation for prayer when you find yourself helpless and fighting hopelessness. In that moment, I could not hold back the tears, fearful of the path I thought might be ahead of us. Then God brought to mind a doctor in Atlanta whom I had seen for a lump in my breast several years before. I knew that if he came to my mind after all these years, God must be telling me to call him. I felt a small glimmer of hope, and I made the call. It was nothing short of a miracle that he agreed to see my dad. The problem we now faced was getting him out of the hospital in Chattanooga to his office in Atlanta as soon as possible, so we checked my dad out of the hospital in the middle of the night without the approval of his doctors. I felt like some kind of criminal, although of course we signed a release. Early the next day we headed to Atlanta, all of us piled into my tiny car. I can still picture my dad's face as we drove away from the home he had worked all his life to have. It was awful. I silently prayed, "God, please. Please, PLEASE let him come home again!"

By this time, I was very active in our church, teaching high school students and serving every opportunity I had. I didn't realize how deeply I felt that God owed me for serving Him so faithfully until God answered my prayers in a way I didn't expect. I prayed that God would heal my dad so he could go home, and that's exactly what He did—but God chose to heal him and take him to his home in heaven, not his earthly home. Dad never returned to the home he loved so much in Chattanooga. One month from the day of his diagnosis, Dad was healed and home, and I know he wouldn't want to come back here.

Nothing on this earth can compare to what is prepared for us in heaven. But as wonderful as I knew it must be for him, the knowledge that he was in heaven, free from pain, did not take away the heartache of missing him. I had watched my dad, this strong man I respected, slowly be reduced to someone who depended on me to change his diapers. I knew God was merciful by taking him home from all of the sickness and pain, but I still had to deal with the fact that God did not answer my prayers the way I wanted.

I was doing everything God asked me to do; why didn't He do what I wanted?

I was far too spiritual to admit this at the time, so I stuffed it. When anyone asked how I was doing, I would reply with "I'm so thankful he's in heaven and cancer-free." Although I wasn't lying, it was certainly not the whole truth. I was upset with God for not performing how I thought a good God would perform. I have learned the hard way that if you stuff your bitterness and anger, it will eventually come out and destroy you.

As time passed, I started to become depressed. God was blessing us financially, and my children were wonderful, but I couldn't appreciate all of the gifts God had given me. I hated my life, and it was because I was blinded by the bitterness I carried from what He did not do. Howard was working long hours, so our time together was short. It didn't take long for my depression and bitterness to convince me that life would be better alone, where I could do what I wanted. At this time, not one person knew how unhappy I was because I had gotten really good at pretending to be happy. Besides, as a Christian, I was told I should be thankful in all things. So I buried my emotions until I became so miserable I couldn't keep them in anymore.

It was during this period that I decided I wanted to leave Howard, and my sister's pastor asked me a life-altering question: "Do you ever want to look back and wonder what God would have done if you had trusted and obeyed Him?" The Holy Spirit burned those words on my heart. I knew I had to obey God and ask Him to heal my marriage.

It was hard, and it took a long time, but God healed my bitter heart and my broken marriage. I love God with all my heart, and I love my sweet Howard more now than I did the day I married Him. My children and grandchildren all love God, and He has miraculously given me a family I do not deserve. God, in His grace and mercy, has restored and redeemed my life.

What does all of this have to do with training? The pain and heartache I experienced during the death of my dad and through that difficult time in my marriage was a training ground for my spiritual race. God led me to seek the truth that is written in the pages of His Word. God used my life circumstances to teach me to seek Him and trust His Spirit to empower me to live the life God called me to.

The first passage God used to train me was Genesis 3. There I read about how God placed Adam and Eve in a beautiful paradise, with all their needs perfectly met, and gave them one rule: not to eat the fruit from the tree of the knowledge of good and evil. It seems like it would not be difficult to avoid one tree when you live in a perfect, beautiful paradise, but one day Eve began to listen to the lies of Satan. She should have started running when the conversation started, but she didn't. Satan awakened in her a desire to be like God, and so she and Adam disobeyed and ate the fruit.

Even though Adam and Eve are our ancient ancestors, we are not exempt from the consequences of their choice to live by their own rules and ignore the one rule God gave them. One rule, one sin, and now every person born thereafter suffers the repercussions of their tragic choice. We have followed in their footsteps: we want to be like God.

When I got mad at God for not doing what I asked Him to do, in effect, I was saying that I knew better than Him. I wanted to be God! But He still gently uses every possible situation and circumstance to train me as His child so that I surrender to His will and allow Him to be God of Dot Bowen. God's training to teach me who He is and who I am has not been an easy program. I still struggle with feeling I know more than God does about how life should be for myself and for the people I love. It's not easy to surrender my will to His. It was even difficult for Jesus. He, too, struggled with His will in Gethsemane, praying until blood flowed down His brow as He asked God to remove the cup of suffering He was about to face. Jesus prayed until He was able to say, "Not My will but Your will be done." If Jesus needed to spend hours in prayer to surrender to the Father's will, I surely need to spend my entire lifetime in prayer!

Training to survive the race God has set for us will never be easy. But without understanding the truth of who God is as written throughout the Bible, we will spend the race wanting to give up with every step and eventually become bitter that God asked us to run in the first place. Remember all those Disney e-mails I ignored? Well, the same is true of Scripture. God has left us His Word to encourage us to run the race He has set for us. As Timothy said, the Bible is useful for teaching us, for helping us understand what we get wrong and how to correct it, and for training us in righteousness. (2 Timothy 3:16). None of it is very fun, nor is it easy. But it is *vital*.

You were created for a purpose, but how would you know this if you never read Psalm 139? How would you know God has a plan for your life unless you read it in Jeremiah 29:11? How would you know Jesus loved you enough to die for you unless you read it in the Gospels? God is so interested in helping us understand how to know Him that He has protected His Word over thousands of years so we could have access to it.

Not one time did Jesus say we would live problem-free. What He did say is that He will walk with us through the problems and give us the power to endure.

Had I known this, I might have understood that God's love and power is greater than my pain. I might have known to pray that God would do what is best for my dad instead of what I thought was best. If I had known the truth about the heart of God, I would have understood that God created the world without sin, sickness, and evil, but we opened that door when Adam and Eve chose to believe the lie that God was withholding something good from them.

I know now that God has created me for a purpose, and He has called me to run the race He has set for me. After failing miserably in my spiritual race, I finally started to train by studying His Word and by seeking Him above all else. I have learned in my training that He asks me to live so that I display His glory and power. His desire is for others to live free from all the lies they have believed as well. He wants us to be able to discern the truth and reject the lies that entangle us.

When I look back on my half marathon experience, I know it would have been totally different if I had trained and learned the rules of competing in a race. When I agreed to run in something, I should have researched what was expected of me. Not only would my experience of running each mile have been different, I would have had a different outcome. If I had taken a small amount of advice from Disney, I would have known what to do and what not to do. If you enjoy running, I'm sure you are shaking your head at my naïveté. Just you wait; it gets worse.

I didn't determine the length of the course, the direction of the race, or all the intricate details. Disney did that. Likewise, in the race God has set for me, He determines every detail within the journey, and He sets the course I must travel. For a long time I believed the lie that it was up to me to determine the outcome of this life.

However, I'm not God, and I cannot control the outcome.

Our choices can determine how much we enjoy life, and they can certainly determine the pain we may experience as a result of them, but being trained in the truth of Scripture helps us to know that the Christian life is not a life to be lived; it is Christ living His life in us. Over time, Jesus kindly trained me in this truth. As long as I'm living on planet earth, I will have to live in the presence of sin, deception, and every form of evil. This is my cross to bear. How wonderful that Jesus overpowered this evil on His cross, and each step I walk with Him is a step in victory!

Jesus has offered the best training program there is, and His truth empowers us to run the race without becoming weary and wanting to give up. It's not an easy training program, but it sure is freeing! In Jesus there is joy, peace, life, and freedom. Freedom to live the life He has created tor us. Freedom to run the race perfectly designed for us. Spiritual training in knowing God's truth is the greatest resource for living the life He desires for us to live. I have found that the life we long to live is the life Jesus died to give us. Life with Him is the best life!

An athlete is not crowned unless he competes
according to the rules.
2 TIMOTHY 2:5

There are very few days when I don't talk with someone who is so discouraged in their Christian life that they are tempted to give up and walk away from God. Why do so many Christians feel so hopeless when they know the God of hope? Why are so many Christians feeling anxious and struggling with fear when they know the God of peace? Could it be they have tried to follow Jesus according to their own rules? Unless you have been trained in the truth of God's Word, you will never win— or even enjoy—the life God has purposed for you. God created us and died to give us life with Him, but we will not know how to live as His children if we don't learn to live by His rules. My greatest regrets have come from living by my rules, but I have never regretted living by God's rules.

If we are going to run and win, we must be trained in the knowledge of who God is and embrace who He created us to be.

Father, may I be reminded every time I feel like I'm running alone that You have promised in Your Word to never leave or forsake me. Teach me Your ways that I might know You more and love You more every day. It is in You, oh God, that I find freedom, hope, and contentment. Please expose all the lies that I have embraced and replace each lie with Your unfailing truth. I love You Jesus, and I'm learning how much You love me.

When You Don't Know What to Do, Go Shopping

For in Christ Jesus you are all sons of God, through faith. For as many of you as were baptized into Christ have put on Christ.

GALATIANS 3:26-27

got off the phone with Christy and sat staring into space, wondering, *What am I going to do?*

Had it really been a whole year since Christy first called to ask me to sign up for the half marathon? Twelve whole months had passed, and during that time the half marathon had been the last thing on my mind. Christy, in her sweet and encouraging way, tried to ease my anxious heart by saying, "Mom, you will do just fine." How she was so confident was beyond me, but I appreciated it greatly in the moment. I was supposed to leave in a few days to run a half marathon and I had no idea how. I didn't even have a clue how many miles were in a half marathon, much less how to actually run those miles. I was fighting off a full-on panic attack when I suddenly had a BRILLIANT idea: I should go shopping! I started to think about our family vacation and that amazing spa I would be enjoying right after the race. It gave me a little boost, and I thought, *I may not have trained to run, but I can LOOK like a runner!*

That's all it took.

I researched where the nearest running store was, grabbed my purse, and out the door I went. I had never been in the Peach Running Store, but in my heart, I knew this was going to be a great day to shop there. As I was driving, I decided I wasn't going to stress over not training anymore. Instead, I was going to make this a fun race and a great family vacation. Trying not to think about what I had not done, I made a plan for what I could do. I decided to buy each of us matching running clothes. I thought this was a brilliant idea and that Cara, my youngest daughter who was also running with us, might want to join Christy and me in our matching running fashion statement.

I called her to cast my beautiful vision of matching mother-daughter running apparel—and was met with silence. Long silence. I'm not sure how long it took Cara to speak, but it was long enough to cast a shadow of doubt on my grand vision. Maybe she wasn't excited to dress like her mother. She finally said with a kind voice, "Mom . . . DO NOT buy me matching running clothes." I told her it was fine, but I made sure she knew Christy and I would be wearing cute and fun running outfits without her. We hung up and I thought, *Well, my goodness! She's just not any fun. I* was so excited over the thought of new running gear and my family vacation that I was not going to allow her sensible attitude to discourage ME from looking like a model in the newest running magazine!

I finally reached the running store, where a very nice man approached me to ask if he could help me with anything. I told him that yes, in fact, I needed a lot of help! I wanted to buy two of everything because my daughter and I were going to have matching outfits to run in Disney's half marathon in a few days. I thought the salesperson would be so excited to hear this news. I don't know how long he had been in sales, but right after I mentioned leaving in a few days, he didn't appear to be very excited to sell me anything. I thought he needed about as much training on how to be a salesperson as I did on how to be a runner. He stood staring at me and finally said, "Oh, so you are a runner?" I quickly replied, "No, I'm not a runner! That's why I need you to help me." I didn't think that he was listening to me, because he asked me again if I was a runner. I reassured him that I was no runner. I'm not sure if I was more irritated by the strange way he was looking at me or because I didn't have all day to explain to this salesperson the ins and outs of my not being a runner. I realized I'd need to take matters into my own hands if I was going to find matching clothes for Christy and me. He couldn't get a clear understanding of why I wanted to buy running clothes if I was not a runner. I had the urge to get in his face and say, "LISTEN TO ME. I'M NOT A RUNNER, I'M A CUSTOMER! FOR THE LOVE . . . SELL ME SOMETHING!" But I didn't think Jesus would be too pleased with this course of action, so I decided against it.

It crossed my mind that perhaps my husband or Cara had called this guy and suggested he should discourage me from spending a lot of money on running shorts I would never wear again. Despite his awkward stares, I still felt the need to explain, in detail, that I was going to run a half marathon at Disney World, and that afterward I was going to enjoy our family vacation. I asked him once again what I needed to buy so I could look like a runner. As nicely as he could, he replied, "Nothing." *Excuse me? Did he say nothing?* He explained to me that because my race was that weekend, it wasn't wise to buy new clothes and shoes before running.

I thought he was kidding, or at least trying to go on break, because NOT buying cute new running outfits seemed ridiculous to me. At this point he seemed confident that I was not a runner, and that I needed professional counseling. I continued looking around the store until he finally realized I was not leaving until I had two of everything. I may not have been a runner, but I certainly planned to look like one. Before I knew it, I had two pairs of running shorts, two t-shirts, two pairs of socks, one pair of running shoes, a cute fanny pack, and almost anything and everything I thought I would need to finish the race and begin my family vacation. I remember finding the nerve to actually ask him if I was missing anything he felt would be essential to running. He mentioned this stuff called "Body Glide."

Body Glide is a stick of some kind of substance that a runner puts on certain parts of her body to keep clothing and . . . ahem . . . fat from rubbing together and irritating the skin while she runs. I looked at the small stick of Body Glide and wondered how many sticks I'd need to cover this non-running body. I decided to buy all he had. I can remember getting in the car and heading home, as happy as I could be with all my new clothes and what felt like a truckload of Body Glide. I had enough to glide for days, or at least enough to glide through Disney. I may not have been a trained runner, but I certainly had everything I needed to look like one!

The next few days passed by at bullet speed, and then our entire family met at the airport, excited to be together for our vacation—and the half marathon, of course. You could feel Christy and Cara's excitement about the race. I can't say I was as excited as they were, but I was beyond excited to have a few days to enjoy my sweet family.

When we arrived at the Grand Floridian Resort, we were told we needed to pick up our runner's packets with our numbers and a few other items we might enjoy during the race. I was overwhelmed when we entered the room filled with so many other runners. Just being among all those others in the room immediately made me feel like a runner even though I had never run a mile, or trained, or desired to be a runner. For that moment, I felt the excitement and thought, *I love runners! I wish I was one!*

It was hard to get to sleep that night. My mind was racing, and I was still on a high from being in the room with all those runners. I knew I had to get up at 4:30 a.m. to get the Body Glide over every part of my body. When morning came, I put on the Glide, donned my new shoes and new running clothes, and met up with the girls to head toward the starting line. Because I had gotten up so early, I told the girls I needed a cup of coffee. Christy and I looked so cute in our matching outfits and, for a fleeting moment, I really *felt* like a runner. How hard could it be to run a half marathon, anyway? I had every intention of asking how many miles were actually in a half marathon, but I was too busy looking cute and finishing my coffee.

I had no idea what it would take to run this half marathon, but I was surely dressed for the part. I found out the hard way that dressing like a runner did NOT make me a runner. As the saying goes, "Being in a coop doesn't make you a chicken."

I have also learned something else the hard way: you can sit in a church, but that doesn't make you a faithful follower of Jesus. Just as I dressed like a runner to cover up my lack of training and fit in with everyone around me, I dressed myself in religious activities to cover up my lack of training as a follower of Jesus. I didn't want my church friends to know I didn't know how to be a good Christian, so I covered up my insecurities by saying "Yes" to every volunteer position at the church. I thought if I went to church every Sunday, attended neighborhood Bible studies, and volunteered to help the poor, everyone would think I was a good Christian. I pretended so long that I started to believe God was impressed with me.

I had been in church since I was a teenager, but I didn't read the Bible until I was married with children. It wasn't until I was failing miserably at trying to be the "good" Christian that I truly desired to know what the Bible said about how to follow Jesus. I had heard preachers on television talk about how great it was to be a Christian. They said that if I had faith, God would give me whatever I asked. They made Jesus sound like Santa Claus. I could give Him my list of wants, and He would fulfill the desires of my heart. Life on earth would be just like heaven.

It doesn't take long to realize that life on earth is not anything like heaven. If it is, we are in trouble! Jesus was not kidding when He said, "In the world you will have tribulation." (John 16:33) I had been told if I had Jesus, life would be good, but my life experience told me that was a lie! My reality did not match my theology.

This really became clear through my dad's death. I had finally turned to God in prayer during my moment of desperation, but then things did not turn out according to my prayers. When my dad wasn't able to enjoy his earthly home again, I was angry with God that I didn't get my way. But I didn't know how angry I was until I began fighting depression. I could cover up my disappointment with God for a while by staying busy. No one would be able to guess I was mad at God if I just kept moving and kept doing. I was so good at covering up my true feelings that even I started to believe I was ok. But you can't stuff your feelings in for too long before they find an escape. The more I covered up my true feelings, the more depressed I became. Eventually, I didn't even want to get out of bed. I was running from everyone I loved, including Jesus, because I felt like He had abandoned me.

God wanted to have a real, authentic, personal relationship with me, and this would never be possible until I stopped covering up my broken heart with busyness and came clean before God. But I was afraid to tell God I was mad at Him. What if He got mad at me and decided to punish me with more pain and suffering? I tried to cover up my true feelings by saying and doing what I thought a good Christian should. I was operating under the misguided notion that God didn't already know what I was hiding. Finally, several months after my dad's death, I realized I wasn't being honest with friends, family, God, and most of all, myself.

Hiding behind "doing" for God instead of just being honest with God is as futile as hiding your real status as a runner behind new running clothes. God looks at us from the inside out, not the other way around. I couldn't cover up my bitterness by going to church. Jesus could see behind my religious cover-up, and He was not impressed. The more I desired to be close to Him, the more distant I felt from Him. That is, until I stopped pretending and removed the clothing of religious activity.

There's nothing we can do to hide the condition of our hearts from God. We can sit in church every time the doors open and hide behind all manner of religious activity, all the while carrying a heart full of bitterness. But God sees it. Sometimes we can't even hide it from other people! If you look into the eyes of a woman who is holding bitterness in her heart, you will see a pain that no makeup or plastic surgery can remove. What we think we are hiding is often obvious to the people closest to us. Even if it isn't, we eventually have to come face-to-face with the truth that the only person we're really fooling is ourselves.

Being real before God and submitting to His will is the only thing that will heal our hearts.

The good news is that God loves His children so much that He will expose what we try to cover up and give us the desire to come out of hiding and run to Him. I think the greatest example of this is found in the lives of Adam and Eve in Genesis 3. Let's pick up their story where we left off—after they made the tragic choice to reject God's rule.

We aren't told how long after their disobedience God came looking for them, but we know they ran and hid as soon as they heard God call their names and tried to cover their newly-discovered nakedness by making clothes out of fig leaves. Eve's running career started right after she listened to Satan. I don't know where they thought they could hide from God, but they tried. If hiding in the garden wasn't ridiculous enough, did they think God wouldn't notice their new designer fig-leaf running apparel? No amount of clothing can cover up the emptiness in one's heart. Trust me, I know it all too well! Their lives were never the same. Reality hit when they had to feel the consequences of their sin: Adam and Eve had to leave their home in the garden. Eve felt the excruciating pain of childbirth, Adam had to work the cursed ground, and they both felt the anguish of their son's death.

Jesus' blood on the cross is the only covering for sin.

O LORD, you have searched me and known me! You know when I sit down and when I rise up; You discern my thoughts from afar. You search out my path and my lying down and are acquainted with all my ways.
PSALM 139:1-3

God knows all things, and He loves His children unconditionally. Therefore, there is no need to hide or run from Him. Besides, you will never be able to outrun God. I know, because I've tried! Just as He came looking for Adam and Eve after they sinned. He has been very faithful to seek me and draw me to Himself. I may be able to hide the real me from everyone else around me, but it's impossible to hide from God. He created me and knows everything about me. God is the one who tells me who I am.

We can laugh at Adam and Eve hiding in the garden dressed in fig leaves, but we do the same ridiculous things when we use serving or busyness to hide from God. He loves us for who we are and wants us to be able to do the same. When we can embrace who we are, we can embrace the God who created us. It has taken me years to accept who I am without comparing myself to others. But if a Holy God loves and accepts me for who I am, why should I stress over the acceptance of others? Did you know that it's much easier to please God than it is to please people? At the end of the day, we can find comfort in the truth that God will never leave or forsake us. So, we can confidently say, 'The Lord is my helper; I will not fear; what can man do to me?'" (Hebrews 13:6).

We can only enjoy the race God has set for us if we throw off all the things that might hinder us. We must remove anything that keeps us from becoming the person God created us to be, and this means being honest with God and with ourselves. If we embrace who we are and the life God has marked out for us, we are on the path to enjoying the life God offers.

The journey to freedom begins the moment you accept and embrace who you are.

If you are trying to discover who you really are, and your first thoughts are, *What should I put on? What is my new style as a follower of Jesus?* then here are a few suggestions:

1. For as many of you as were baptized into Christ have put on Christ. (Galatians 3:27)

2. But that is not the way you learned Christ!—
   assuming that you have heard about him and
   were taught in him, as the truth is in Jesus, to put
   off your old self, which belongs to your former
   manner of life and is corrupt through deceitful
   desires, and to be renewed in the spirit of your
   minds, and to put on the new self, created after
   the likeness of God in true righteousness and holi-
   ness. (Ephesians 4:20-24)

3. Therefore, having put away falsehood, let each
   one of you speak the truth with his neighbor, for
   we are members one of another. (Ephesians 4:25)

4. Put on then, as God's chosen ones, holy and beloved,
   compassionate hearts, kindness, humility, meek-
   ness, and patience. (Colossians 3:12)

5. And above all these put on love, which binds everything together in perfect harmony. (Colossians 3:14)

The kind salesperson at the Peach Running Store
wanted to protect me from the pain that new shoes and
clothing would cause while running a half marathon.
See, he knew I wasn't a runner . . . and he was right. My
feet ached throughout the entire race. And the large
amount of Body Glide I had applied to my body did not
keep my new clothing from rubbing against my skin.
He knew what was best for me because he was trained
and experienced.

I should have listened!

Father, I thank You that I no longer have to depend upon my righteousness to receive Your forgiveness. Instead, I put on the righteousness of Jesus that He offers to each of His children. I'm in awe of Your goodness and mercy that allows me to enter into Your presence. I believe by faith that because of Jesus' righteousness I can enter into the presence of a Holy God. Thank You for listening to me and allowing me to make my requests known to You. I wait upon You. Oh, Jesus, how I love and worship You!

Everyone Needs to Start Somewhere

Brothers, I do not consider that I have made it my own. But one thing I do: forgetting what lies behind and straining forward to what lies ahead.

PHILIPPIANS 3:13

can't remember every detail about the half marathon, but the scene at the starting line is clearly etched in my mind.

I have never seen so many eager runners in my life. We were given an individual runner's number, as well as a group number to help guide us to our place at the starting line. Like most larger races, Disney had divided people into brackets based on estimated speed. The fastest runners start first, and then starting times go in waves. Thousands of runners from around the world, women and men, old and young, all took their places and lined up to begin their race at their appointed time.

I stood in utter amazement as I watched the runners around me stretching. It almost looked like Cirque du Soleil was performing! I can confidently say that my body has never once bent into the positions these people were contorting their bodies into. I was impressed with all the unique stretches and warm-up exercises that so many people were engaged in before the race. As for me, my warm-up was the coffee in my hand, and it had a big job to do—keeping me awake.

I turned to talk with my girls and, sure enough, there they were, bending over, raising their legs, and twisting their bodies as they got ready to start. I wondered, *What is wrong with these people?!* I could think of nothing worse than stretching this early in the morning, especially before I was about to exert so much energy running however many miles this was. Christy asked if I was going to stretch, and I informed her that if I were to put my body in those positions, I would never recover, much less run. The girls laughed, but I was serious. My body does not have the ability to turn into a pretzel.

As we were waiting, Christy happened to mention that if I did not arrive at a certain mile marker by a particular time, a volunteer called a "sweeper" would come pick me up and take me to wait for them at the finish line. WHAT?!! No sir. No one was going to pick me up or take me anywhere! I signed up for this half marathon to run, not ride, and I would be running the entire race on my own, thank you very much. Who knew a fun place like Disney would have so many rules in their half marathon? I think this may have been the first time Christy realized I truly knew nothing about this race.

Christy said, "Mom, you can't take all day to run." I reassured her that I would be fine and would meet her at the finish line having run ALL my miles. I wanted Christy and Cara to run their race, and I would run mine. Christy reminded me of the monitor on my shoe that would send a text to the family when I crossed the finish line, and we made a plan for where to meet after the race. Suddenly we looked ahead and realized that the group had started to move—the race had begun! I knew this was it. I was focused, determined to run by my own rules. My strong will kicked in, and I knew I would run fast enough to ensure that no one picked me up.

Just being in the crowd brought a sense of excitement. When I finally stepped over the starting line, my heart was racing! It was my turn. You see, every runner has to start at the starting line. You can crawl, walk, or run across the line, but until you move forward, you can't experience the joy and excitement of the race. The start is crucial.

The truth I have discovered in running the race of life is that God has a plan for me, a course for me to run. I can trust Him to lead me down the path He chooses, or I can reject His plan. For years I tried to pave the path I wanted without considering God's will for me. I heard other people's success stories and saw what always appeared to be their perfect lives. I thought I could be happy if I had what they had. Oh, how often we wait for our lives to start while longing for someone else's! It's the poison of "if only . . . "

"If only I had her husband,"
"If only I had their financial status,"
"If only I had that family,"
"If only I had her looks,"
If only . . . when do they stop?

As long as we live with the "if only" mind-set, we will never be content living with what is.

This is not to say we should stop trying to improve our situation or live better. God wants to us to live victoriously through His power, and that means daily discipline and improvement. What I'm saying is that there are some things we cannot control, circumstances in our lives that we must trust God to change while asking Him to give us the strength and patience to live and run the race He has asked us to run. Over the years, I have heard some amazing stories from women whose lives took them down paths they never believed they would have to travel. I have sat beside moms whose children were fighting cancer. I have talked with women who have been unfaithful to their husbands or were victims of their husband's unfaithfulness. I have listened to women who were controlled by the shame and despair of their past regrets, who longed to be free from the bondage of their own choices. None of us can escape this life without experiencing some level of pain, whether it is physical or emotional. Every life has a unique story that needs telling, a race to be run.

God has given us the power to choose how we will approach life's journey, but He determines the path. Every follower of Jesus will be asked to run in her own lane, down the path that God has paved specifically for her. He gives all of us different dreams, hopes, passions, and purpose, and we're uniquely designed for the path He places us on. Nothing is more frustrating than comparing our race with someone else's, our struggles or achievements against someone else's. In God's Kingdom, the starting line begins at the foot of Jesus' cross. His death purchased and clothed every runner with grace, mercy, and forgiveness, and now He offers us a life purpose. I believe that until God calls us home, He offers us the privilege of being used by Him to live out His purpose.

Just like the thousands of runners taking their places around the starting line for the half marathon, we come from many different places and backgrounds, starting at different paces and different times. We all have been given a path to run. Nobody can run my race; that's uniquely mine! And I cannot run someone else's race.

We can't run the race God has for our children, our husbands, or anyone we love. God has established their courses, just as He has established ours.

In all of life there is a "letting go" of one thing and a moving forward to "grab hold" of what is next.

If we are to run the race God has for us, we must let go of the past and embrace the life God offers.

We must let go of comparing ourselves to others and embrace who we are. In Psalm 139, King David wrote, "For you (God) formed my inward parts; you knitted me together in my mother's womb. I praise you, for I am fearfully and wonderfully made" (verse 13-14). When was the last time you praised God for the way you are made? God has masterfully created you for His purposes. We had no choice about where we were born or who our parents would be, but God determined these things for us and uses them to help shape our journeys. We must embrace who we are and where we have been so we can move forward to what is next.

You have no idea what God can do if you are willing to surrender to His will.

In 2012, my son, Scott, founded Champions United, an organization that uses soccer as a tool for building into the lives of children in Uganda. Champions United is in a small town outside of Kampala. The organization aims to equip and teach men how to become leaders of integrity and models how to be a follower of Jesus through mentoring, both peer-to-peer and coach-to-player. It is a faith ministry built on intentional mentoring through the sport of soccer.

For over five years, I prayed for the opportunity to see firsthand what God is doing through his work, but there was just one problem: I hate to fly. This is an especially difficult challenge because the flight from Atlanta to Uganda is 24 hours. But after five years, I knew I could be brave enough to get on a plane and see in person what I had only heard about.

When we arrived, the children were having what we might call Vacation Bible School. They were making crafts, playing games, and listening to the story of David and Goliath. The theme for the week was courage. I found myself feeling guilty for needing the courage to fly to Uganda as I looked at these children who have such courage while living in slums without electricity and food. I could not hold back my tears when we drove into the many green fields filled with the laughter of children who are running their own races. The reality is that I did not choose to live in America, and these precious children did not choose to live in Uganda. It is what it is. I'm not a better person because I live in Atlanta, and they are not less because they live in the slums of Uganda. God loves each of us, and He has provided us with everything we need to succeed in our own race. These beautiful children showed me what it looks like to run in a way that brings glory to God in ALL circumstances. I want to have the courage to do the same.

You see, it's not where we start that matters, but how we run and finish our own race. God is not going to hold me accountable for someone else's race, but you better believe I will be responsible for running and living the life He has asked me to live. Simply put, I'm to live my life, not try to live someone else's. God created each of us for a purpose, and it is our responsibility to run in obedience to what He has given us. If the sweet children in Uganda can sing praises to God in the circumstances they have been given, I can surely sing in mine.

Several years ago, I was challenged with this question: "What would the world miss if you never told your story?" We all have a story worth telling. I realized that God wanted me to tell this story—His story of hope, forgiveness, and redemption in my life. I have traveled down many winding roads and faced many uphill battles. I have dreaded the storms in life and was quick to ask God to remove the rugged path of pain. I have made choices I regret and choices I'm thankful for. I have come to many crossroads, not knowing which way would be the best path for me. I have been down paths that led to regret and paths that led to peace. I have chosen my own way, and I have surrendered my paths to God. The journey I have traveled has become my story, a small part of God's beautiful story.

So, what is your story? No one can tell it better than you. Someone, somewhere needs to hear that their life matters, that there is purpose to all this pain and suffering. A life that understands despair can experience hope. In fact, it's a central piece of the story for many of us. I've been so surprised when God takes what little I offer and uses it to bring hope to the hopeless. As children of God, we all start somewhere, and we all have a story that only we can tell. Never underestimate the power of story in a life changed by God.

As I looked at all the runners in the half marathon, I saw men and women with hopes and dreams of a better life. As I looked at the beautiful, brown-eyed children in Uganda, I saw their hopes and dreams of a better life. As I look at the people surrounding me everyday, I know there's someone who needs to hear that God is their hope for a better life. In Him is the answer to all our dreams.

God wants to weave His story into your story. What is your story? Who are you surrounded by that might need someone to encourage them to run their own race?

_____

What would the world miss if you never told your story?

_____

Father, thank You that nothing can separate me from Your love. I want to take this opportunity to offer You all my sins, my regrets, my failures, my successes, and everything I possess to use for Your glory. In Romans 8 You said all things work together for our good and Your glory. Never once have You said all things are good, but that You will make all things good. May I be careful to give You all the glory for all You have done in and through me. I love You, Jesus, and I'm so thankful for all things in my life that will bring hope to someone You send my way.

Thirsty

Jesus said to her, "Everyone who drinks of this water will be thirsty again, but whoever drinks of the water that I will give him will never be thirsty again. The water that I will give him will become in him a spring of water welling up to eternal life."

JOHN 4:13-14

The sun was well on its way up. Even though it was January, the weather felt like a beautiful spring day. Florida is notorious for random showers popping up unexpectedly, but if the weather report was correct for race day, it was going to be one of those perfect Florida spring days in the middle of January. A perfect cup of coffee, a perfect day to run a half marathon, and a perfect day to enjoy the park with the family. LET THE RACE BEGIN!

Since I had not trained, I had no frame of reference for how long it would take a non-runner like myself to finish. If I didn't know how many miles were in a half marathon, I certainly didn't know how to estimate my finish time. As the crowd of runners gradually began moving and the race got underway, I waved goodbye to my family and slowly began to run. I'm not sure exactly how long we had been running when I noticed people stopping to take pictures with a few Disney characters. I couldn't believe people were willing to just stop like that. I didn't want a picture; I wanted to finish so I could get a massage at the Grand Floridian spa!

As we continued, I started to see people stopping along the road to go to the bathroom. There were rows upon rows of porta potties along the way, but the lines to use them were long. Not being a big fan of running anyway, I figured if I were to stop for any length of time I would never start again. Of course, I could choose not to take a picture with a Disney character, but if my body said it was time for a bathroom break, I wouldn't be able to control that for very long. I knew stopping would only take more time, and that put me at risk for getting picked up by a sweeper. That was NOT going to happen.

Somewhere along the way I had a brilliant idea. I didn't know anything about running, but I did know that putting water into my body would mean water would have to come out, and that was a risk I couldn't take. So, I made the decision not to drink water. This seemed like a perfectly logical choice at the time. After the race, I learned it is very important to be hydrated while running 13.1 miles, especially on a warm day in Central Florida. Every time I share this story, someone always tells me that not only are you to drink water while running, you are to start drinking water days before the race to stay hydrated. Me? I was buying cute new running outfits the days before, and I started my race with a cup of coffee in hand, which happens to be a natural diuretic. I'm not really that into drinking water anyway. It made perfect sense to me that I should finish the race and then I could have all the water I wanted while sitting in a luxury spa.

I had already made two significant decisions at the beginning of my race. First, I would run at a pace that would guarantee I wouldn't be swept up to the finish line. Second, I would wait until after I finished the race to drink water so I wouldn't need to go to the restroom. I felt confident in my decisions, so my strong will kicked in and off I ran.

I don't recall how long I had been running when I started to get really tired. I passed many water stations and several volunteers handing small paper cups of water to runners. I took some of them, and each time I splashed the water on my body as a coolant without putting a drop of it in my mouth. I had no idea how many more miles I had left, but I needed something to get me to the finish line. If I couldn't drink water and I couldn't slow down, what could I do to get a little more energy? Suddenly I remembered that I had put a 2-point Weight Watcher's protein bar in the cute fanny pack I'd bought from that poor man at the running store.

I slowed down just a little to get the bar out, and then I eagerly took a bite. I have enjoyed these protein bars for years, but in that moment, I had never tasted anything so awful in my life. It was as if I was trying to chew rocks. The texture was bad enough, but it was the horrible taste in my mouth that made me gag. I didn't have enough saliva to even chew it up and swallow it. I decided that when I came to the next water station, I would take a few sips and swish it around just enough to get the bar taste out of my mouth. And I did just that; I took a couple sips, swished it around, and spit the rest of the water on the ground. I was quite proud of myself for getting the awful taste out of my mouth without swallowing any water.

With every passing mile marker, I found myself getting more and more exhausted. I wanted so badly to stop, but I knew that if I did, even for a second, the race would be over for me. I didn't want to disappoint the girls, so I kept running, even though the thought of finishing seemed as impossible as climbing Mount Everest. I knew I had to push through, but by this point I didn't know if I could. I couldn't remember how many miles I had already run or how many were left. I just knew I was tired, I hated running, and I WAS THIRSTY! Still I refused the water that was literally being handed to me. The fear of not finishing, and my selfish pride that had me run the race on my own terms, came at a costly price.

That day I learned what it means to be physically thirsty, but I already knew what it means to be spiritually thirsty.

Both have the potential to kill you.

The word "thirsty" can be expressed in many different ways: being anxious, greedy, hungry, parched, and impatient . . . longing, lusting, yearning, and dying for something. These are all forms of thirst. Some of these words take me back to my middle and high school years, to the days before I decided to follow Jesus when I had a longing and thirst for someone to love and accept me for who I was. I just wanted to be loved unconditionally. As I've said, I do think my parents loved me unconditionally, but they had a hard time expressing their love. No matter how much someone loves you, if they never tell you that, more than likely you'll have a hard time believing it. When there is an unmet need or desire, people will sometimes do whatever it takes to find a way to quench their thirst, even if it means making unwise decisions.

I was married with children before I heard the actual words "I love you" from my parents, and even then, I was the first to say it. I had often heard that if you want something, you should give it away, and then it will come back to you. I'm not sure if this applies to everything, but this principle is why I made a commitment to always tell my mom I loved her. The first time I said it, silence that felt like hours filled the room before she said, "I love you, too." Over time it got easier for her, and sometimes she even said I love you before I did.

My dad wasn't big on expressing his love either. I remember leaving my parents' home one Christmas day to drive to Arkansas to spend Christmas with Howard's family. As we were leaving, my dad handed me a small, wrinkled piece of paper. I can remember to this day how anxious I was to read his note. I read just two sentences, written in his handwriting:

> *I'm not too good at words but I wanted to tell you that I love you very much and thank you for making this the best Christmas I have ever had. I thank God for you.*
> **—Daddy**

There are no sweeter words to me (other than God's Word, of course) than these that my dad gave to me. This was the first time I heard my dad say, "I love you," and he had to write it in a note to do so. And he thanked God for me. I had no idea my dad prayed, much less for me. I cried all the way from Chattanooga to West Memphis, Arkansas. To this day, that letter sits in a frame on my desk, where I see it every morning. It was not long after he gave me this handwritten love note that he went home to be with Jesus, so I treasure it. I have a few antiques in my home, nice furniture, and some jewelry, but if a fire breaks out, his letter will be the first thing I grab.

To be loved and accepted is a thirst everyone
seeks to quench.

I have spent hours upon hours meeting with and teaching teenage girls, and never once has there been a girl who hasn't expressed a desire—a desperate thirst—to feel loved by her parents. What does a young girl do when her need for love and acceptance is not met? Whatever it takes to find someone to quench her thirst.

That is what the encounter Jesus had with the Samaritan woman was all about. You can find her story in John chapter 4. There's no doubt in my mind that she was NOT looking for a husband. She had already been married five times. When she met Jesus, she was living with another man, someone I believe she hoped would quench her thirst to be loved.

I can identify with that. The memories I have of my high school years consist mostly of a broken heart. I was the typical teenage girl who wanted the attention of every guy she thought was cute. I hate to admit this, but I flirted with every guy who glanced my way. I went to school every day with one thing on my mind, and it was not getting an education. I had a thirst to feel pretty, loved, and valued, and I wanted the attention of any cute boy.

Though I was very active in softball, band, and majorettes, I look back over those high school years and realize that although I was friends with all the popular students, I never felt good enough to be their friend. The more I compared myself to them, the less I measured up to their standards. I not only felt unloved and unaccepted, I felt stupid. I wanted to be loved, respected, and to have a life of significance, yet I had a hard time loving and respecting myself, so why would I expect someone else to? The problem with desiring these things is that I cannot make anyone love, respect, or value me. None of us can.

The desire to quench our thirsty and longing hearts is as real a need as the desire to drink water in order to quench our physical thirst.

God has planted that longing to be loved deep in our hearts, and He alone can fill it.

But we have to choose to accept His love.

The Samaritan woman wanted to take Jesus up on His offer to give her living water that would help her never thirst again. Wouldn't we all? Most of us seek everything and everyone to quench the thirst in our hearts . . . everyone except Jesus. What Jesus told the Samaritan woman is the same thing He tells us—nothing but what He offers will give eternal satisfaction. Just as the woman came to get water from Jacob's well every day, so also we continue to quench our desires with self-made wells. We drink, then find ourselves thirstier than before. How many times do we seek after the wells called People's Approval, Someone's Love, Position, Power, and Control?

That's not an exhaustive list of the many wells we seek to quench our thirst, only to be satisfied for a moment. After a while, we stop drinking from these wells and begin to suck the life out of the people we seek to please.

If I'm honest, this is, by far, the hardest chapter I've had to write. I have stopped and closed my computer more times than I can count, just to give my mind a break from these painful memories of my past. My youngest daughter is a great writer, and as I was sharing with her how difficult it has been for me to write this chapter without tears rolling down my cheeks, she said, "What brings tears to the writer brings tears to the reader." If this is true, my heart is sad for all the tears you may have shed reading this chapter.

Please don't hear me say I had a bad childhood. My parents may not have expressed their love in ways I knew how to receive, but I knew in my heart that they loved me deeply. I found out later that neither of my parents experienced that kind of tenderness in their childhood either. My mom lost her mother at an early age, so she and her siblings had to become independent much too early. The same was true for my dad. This helped me understand why they weren't quick to say they loved me, but it did not take away my longing to hear words of affirmation and love.

If I, as a desperate teenager looking for love, had lived in today's culture of casual sex and drinking, I shudder to think what I would have done. My thirst to be loved and accepted by the people around me was toxic. The danger of trying to satisfy these desires is the bondage we experience in trying to do for ourselves something only God can do. Without God, our only choice is to look for ways to quench our thirst with human provision. I think this is why Jesus said in no uncertain terms that He alone can satisfy the natural longings of men and women. The God who gave us our desires is the same God who satisfies them.

Several years ago, we were bombarded with the question, "What would Jesus do?" It was printed on everything from bumper stickers to wrist bands. The purpose behind the simple question was to help us stop in the midst of making a decision, ask ourselves what we thought Jesus would have done in a similar situation, and then follow His example. My problem was that I had no idea what Jesus would do! I had to guess a lot, because I didn't really know Him. If we concentrate on what Jesus would do, we can easily miss who Jesus is. I know from experience that nothing can leave you more spiritually thirsty than trying to be like Jesus instead of loving and knowing Jesus.

Of course, we cannot use this as an excuse to disobey the teachings of Jesus. Obedience is essential to living the life God offers. However, I have discovered in my race with Jesus that obedience does not produce love. Instead, as we seek to love God with all of who we are, and as God places His love into our hearts, obedience is the natural by-product. I think this is what Jesus meant when He offered water to the Samaritan woman and said, "If you knew the gift of God, and who it is that asks you for a drink, you would have asked him, and he would have given you living water" (John 4:10). Jesus was the only person who could quench her thirst for love, not her five ex-husbands or the man she was living with.

Only Jesus can satisfy our thirsty souls. So, the question we must ask is why are so many Christians so spiritually thirsty?

The number of people who have walked away from their decision to follow Jesus because of despair and disappointment is alarming. I think our desire to quench our own thirst and drink from our self-made wells is the reason we sometimes feel so hopeless. Remember in the half marathon when I was offered water? Instead of drinking, I splashed it on the outside of my body, trying to find strength from the outside. I thought I could quench my own thirst after the race. I selfishly swished water in my mouth, taking what I thought would bring me value, and spat out valuable, lifesaving water on the ground. I thought I was in control. I had no idea the horrible consequences of not having water in my system. Little did I know that a few more miles would bring me face-to-face with the consequences of my choices. I thought I could decide how to make myself strong. I was wrong.

The desire to be loved, accepted, valued, and significant can only be satisfied when we allow the Spirit of God to fill our thirsty souls. If we seek after anything or anyone to make us feel complete and satisfied, it will only be a matter of time before we find ourselves thirsty and disappointed in life. Thirsty people start to feel desperate and hopeless unless they receive the water only Jesus can provide. I hope you understand what I mean when I say I know what it means to be physically and spiritually thirsty, and that both have the potential to rob me of the life God offers. Did I mention that one of the essentials I purchased at the running store was a water bottle? Yes, I attached a very cute water bottle to my fanny pack. I had all the water I needed right there with me, but I refused to drink.

What about your running story? Have you tried to quench your thirst by seeking the approval of others or looking for love in all the wrong places? Has trying to manage or survive this race called life left you thirsty?

Jesus provides all the water we will ever need to satisfy our thirsty souls.

He says to us as He said to the Samaritan woman, "If you knew the gift of God, and who it is that asks you for a drink, you would have asked him, and he would have given you living water!"

We all are thirsty and long for something. What are the desires of your heart? What are you thirsty for?

A satisfied life in Jesus is available upon request.

Father, please forgive me for the many times I have tried to satisfy the desires of my heart by drinking from man-made wells. Jesus, You have often said that if I would drink from You, You would satisfy the longing of my heart. One thing I know for sure is nothing in this world can satisfy more than a life surrendered to the will of God. I realize You have a purpose and plan for my life, it is You I must run to. Jesus, You are the cup that never runs dry. Give me the wisdom and desire to drink from the truth of who You are and to embrace who You say I am in You. I love You, Jesus!

My Own Cheering Squad

You were running well. Who hindered you from obeying the truth?

GALATIANS 5:7

For the first time since the race began, the fear of having to stop for a restroom break completely left me. I didn't have the energy to think about a bathroom; I was concentrating on the finish line! With each step, I fought discouraging thoughts and doubt. I was so thirsty and tired that I began thinking I may not be able to finish the race. When I was sipping my coffee at the starting line, not finishing wasn't an option. I would not even entertain the thought. Fast-forward many miles into the race without any water, and getting swept up to take a ride to the finish line didn't seem like such a bad idea.

It is in moments like these that I realize my mom and dad's inner struggles are still very much a part of me. My mom and dad were the epitome of the word "survivor." Even though they ultimately lost their battles against cancer, they fought it with every ounce of their beings. Mom and Dad fought through many difficulties throughout their marriage, difficulties I never appreciated or really even understood until I was married. The days I spent with my dad during his cancer treatments and the many nights I got to spend with both my parents in the hospital gave me the opportunity to hear their story of survival. I'm so proud of my parents and consider it the greatest gift to say I am their child. They fought diligently, and their example taught me to never give up.

If I close my eyes even now, I can see that hill I thought I would never have the energy to climb on the path that Disney had mapped out for each runner. As I stared at that hill, my mind was overwhelmed with so many thoughts: *Can I really keep running? Do I have what it takes to do this? What was I thinking, signing up for this race without training? Please, God, let this race be over already!* I just wanted it over, and I wanted water. Well, that and my Disney half marathon gold medal, too!

At my lowest moment in the race, when I could barely run any longer, I started hearing something I couldn't believe. No, it wasn't angels singing. Nor did I hear God whisper, "You can do this!" Instead, I heard cheering from the crowd of people lining the road, spectators cheering on the runners as they passed. I couldn't count the number of people crowding the sidelines because there were so many, but I felt like they were all my best friends. I know one thing: they were precious in my sight! The enthusiasm of the people and the cheers gave me the boost I needed to keep running. It was as if I had been given a shot of adrenaline. We didn't actually know each other, but in my half-delusional, dehydrated mind, I thought they were the greatest people I had ever seen, and here they were cheering *me* to victory! As I passed by, many would hold out their hands and I would slap each one with a smile on my face. I heard them say, "Good job!" or "You can do this!" or "You're almost there, keep running!" Of course, they had no idea if I could actually do it, but their words sounded like a sweet melody in my ears. When someone is fighting discouragement and doubt, words like "You can do it!" are a breath of fresh air, even if those words are uninformed and potentially untrue.

What the cheering crowd did not know was that I did not have even a drop of water in my system or any bit of nourishment to give me the energy to keep running. I had no water and no food, but I did have the applause of the crowd. As I listened to their encouragement to keep running, I felt new energy coursing through my veins. With a few right words at the right time, I was given a new desire to keep running. But there was a (huge) problem—the crowd didn't know they were cheering me on to my destruction, nor did they know what I would face around the corner. Not only did the crowd not know me, they didn't know the choices I had made before and during the race. They didn't know that I chose not to train before the race, or that I was prideful enough to push too far just so I could say I ran the whole way. They didn't know that I chose not to drink anything during the race.

When we are in tough situations in our lives and facing critical decisions, often we listen to the opinions of others before we seek the wisdom of God. Though they are well-intentioned, sometimes other people may not know the choices we made that led us to the difficult place we find ourselves.

Our actions play a critical role in how we run our own race, and they often determine the consequences we experience, both good and bad.

When I'm quick to call my friends for advice without the slightest thought to call on God first, my mind immediately goes to the story of Job in the Bible.

Years ago, I enrolled in a 3-year seminary program with Biblical Training for Christian Leaders, which enabled me to study the Bible in more depth than I had previously. I'll never forget when we came to the book of Job. I had always hated that book because I feared God might mention my name to Satan and allow him to do to me what he did with Job and his family. To my surprise, the class on Job turned out to be my favorite. I discovered that Job is not as much about suffering as it is about a question: Will a man serve God for nothing?

Maybe you are acquainted with Job's story, or maybe you have never even heard of it before. I encourage you to take time to read his entire story. I believe Job's story is relevant in today's world and a great resource for comforting friends when they face adversity, as well as what to expect when friends try to comfort you during difficult circumstances.

The book opens with a conversation between God and Satan, and this conversation is key to the entire book. During this talk God allowed Satan to strip Job of all his blessings, with one rule in place: Satan could not take Job's life. When the news got around town about Job's misfortune, people began to talk. It didn't take long for word to get out that Job's children were killed in a terrible storm and Job lost all his earthly possessions in a very short amount of time. If losing his children and his home weren't devastating enough, soon Job started losing his health. Before Satan launched a full-blown assault on Job, we're told that God had blessed Job with a great deal of wealth and earthly possessions. He was also a man of character, with a spotless reputation in the eyes of all who knew him. But Satan accused Job of only loving God's blessings, not truly loving and worshiping God Himself. It was beyond Satan's comprehension that anyone would worship and love God for who He is, and not just for what He can give. Satan challenged God to remove all His blessings to see what Job was really made of. The enemy was sure Job would curse God once he was stripped of everything he held dear.

When things started to fall apart, Job's wife even turned on him and suggested he curse God and die. Now, I've had my share of frustrations in marriage, but this is another level! I don't think Job's wife would ever be considered a good marriage counselor. Talk about hitting someone while they are down! Unfortunately, Job's wife and friends would be at the top of that list.

Since Job was so respected and popular among the people, it wasn't long before his long-time friends dropped in uninvited . . . and stayed for seven days . . . without saying a single word. Can you imagine knocking on the door of a friend's house after they had encountered their worst nightmare, walking in, taking a seat in their living room, and staying there, quiet, for seven days? It seems unbelievable. If you read further into the book of Job, you discover that their silence was the greatest gift they could have given him, because after seven days they started talking, and it would have been better for all concerned if they had just remained silent.

Job was miserable. His body was wasting away, and he had nothing left except a wife who had given him permission to walk away from his God and die, and friends who were suddenly very anxious to offer their opinions on all this misfortune. You know you are in trouble when someone other than God decides to give you her expert opinion on why God has allowed your suffering. Job's friends—or "cheering squad"—had every theological reason for why he had experienced such heartache. Their advice was based on their limited knowledge. But there was one slight problem: they didn't know about the conversation between God and Satan, and this conversation is the single most important detail in the entire story. As you can imagine, Job was not happy with his friends' advice or religious assumptions. His frustration peaks when they accuse him of sinning, implying that God is punishing him for his disobedience. Job had had it with his so-called "cheering squad" and called them lousy comforters.

After we read all the advice Job's friends freely offered, then God begins to speak. He never answers the "why." Instead, He reminds Job of His power as Creator of the heavens and earth, and how He didn't need the help of Job or His friends in doing so. After reminding Job that He is Almighty God and can do whatever He chooses, God turns the conversation to Job's friends. He reprimands them for speaking on His behalf, because they were incapable of knowing why God allowed Job's circumstances.

There is no one who can explain the actions of God except God Himself.

I would not have wanted to be one of those friends in that moment. At one point, He told the friends to ask Job for forgiveness, and said that if Job was willing to forgive them, then He would, too. Their advice was wrong, their theology was wrong, and their view of God was wrong. As awkward as it was, Job's friends should have just kept silent!

The book of Job teaches us the danger of giving someone advice based on personal experience and human wisdom. Yet how many times do we take the counsel of people before we seek the wisdom of God? How quickly do we call our friends when life falls apart, instead of calling upon God? Sure, it's wise to seek godly counsel, but only after we have first sought God's counsel. If you need wisdom, go to the source of all wisdom. If your "cheering squad" speaks truth from God's Word, listen to what they have to say. If they can only offer their opinions or experiences, just go out for lunch and talk about the weather.

The crowd that was cheering me in my half marathon had no idea what they were really doing when they encouraged me to keep running. They were unaware of the choices and life-altering decisions I had made before and during my race. These choices affected how I was running the race, the dangers I would face at the end, and eventually would affect my family. If you look hard enough and long enough, you will find someone to tell you what you want to hear. Unfortunately, what you want to hear may not be what you need to hear.

It has been over 33 years since the day I looked for someone to give me permission to walk out on my marriage. After stuffing my anger toward God for not healing my dad of cancer, my bitterness eventually spilled out onto Howard and our marriage. It's not surprising that Satan took this opportunity to accuse me of not being who I should have been or who I felt God wanted me to be. I was deeply grieving the loss of my dad, and I was vulnerable to his attack.

It's also not surprising that our greatest struggle as a couple came when we were being faithful to seek God in our personal lives and in our marriage. We longed to trust God with all our hearts, and this is when Satan launched his first attack. Howard had left a high-level job with a large income to start his own business because he felt God was asking him to as an act of obedience. He was the youngest president this company had ever promoted, and under his leadership it was one of the most successful times in the history of this construction company. That was very hard to walk away from. Howard was trying to grow his company, and I was left at home with small kids in a town that I hated. I had never lived outside of Chattanooga, and I hated being away from my mom and sisters. I knew it would not be easy to stay with Howard, but I also knew I had to obey God. To this day the hairs on my arms stand up when I think about the question my sister's pastor asked me: *"Do you want to look back and wonder what God would have done, had you only obeyed Him?"*

NO! No, I do not! The very next Sunday after I met with that pastor, I was at my sister's church, where their new pastor was preaching. This was the man I had planned to meet with, but then my sister advised me to see her old pastor instead. That Sunday the new pastor made the statement that he was not against divorce. I still get chills when I think that if I had spent any time with him, he might have given me an excuse to walk away from my marriage. If I hadn't spoken with the man who believed divorce was not an option, I would not be writing this book—I would be divorced. Where would I be, had I listened to worldly wisdom? Would our kids be bitter? Would they have turned their backs on God? It's not easy to be a single mom, and it's impossible to be happy in disobedience.

I was at a crossroads in my marriage, and the path I chose would determine the course of my journey. I had no idea when I was contemplating leaving my marriage the price I would have to pay. I told a friend how unhappy I was, and she said, "You deserve to be happy and to think about what *you* want." She told me that God wanted me happy and would understand if I had to walk away. She said the kids would understand and, in time, be able to adapt to the divorce. My friend who was cheering me on to do what I wanted was leading me down the road of self-destruction. She truly believed what she was telling me was right, but she could not have been more wrong. I can't express with words how thankful I am to Larry Draper, the pastor who told me the truth even when the truth was not what I wanted to hear.

If you are looking for a way out of anything, you can always find someone who will encourage you to walk in that direction. It's easy to find cheerleaders among a crowd. It's much harder to find true friends who tell you the difficult truth. It's even more rare to find a faithful friend who will pray for you and encourage you to seek God before you start running into dangerous territory. The writer of Hebrews 11 encourages us by listing all the great men and women of the Bible who kept their faith even as they were facing their own death. Reflecting on the "great cloud of witnesses" that these faithful runners are, the writer continues in chapter 12:

> *Therefore, since we are surrounded by so great a cloud of witnesses, let us also lay aside every weight, and sin which clings so closely, and let us run with endurance the race that is set before us.*
> **HEBREWS 12:1**

The stories of these witnesses are written throughout the Bible. When we learn how these great men and women of God ran their race, we can be encouraged to run in such a way that we will win the prize in the end. The only thing we cannot do is run someone else's race. Every once in a while, we may run into someone with a similar story to ours, but no two stories are exactly the same. We cannot compare our race with anyone else's, nor can we expect that God will do for us exactly what He has done for someone else. He will do what is best for each of us, and that means our purposes and paths will be specifically and uniquely designed, in God's loving care, for us individually.

In time, we will be able to encourage people in our lives to run their race with the good news that God will never leave them running alone. The difference between witnesses and cheerleaders is determined by whether they are fellow runners or just spectators. The witnesses in Hebrews 11 are runners who not only finished their race, but kept the faith. The great runners of biblical days are in heaven, celebrating the victory with Jesus and resting in His presence.

Jesus gives us the faith to run, and we can enjoy and feel His applause as we faithfully complete our race.

Remember, God is using difficult circumstances to disciple, train, and protect you as you run. Yes, you can reflect on your past running experiences, learn from your past mistakes, reshape and develop a better strategy, but no one knows exactly what God is doing in your life except God Himself. I lovingly encourage you to choose your cheering section carefully. Whom do you run to for godly advice? Whom do you listen to when you find yourself wanting to give up on life? Where do you go when you need to make some very important decisions?

When Adam and Eve listened to Satan and made the decision to disobey God, He came looking for them with two very powerful questions. He asked Adam and Eve "Where are you?" not because He didn't know; He asked because He wanted them to be fully aware of where they were. He wanted them to confess where they had run to and what they had done. After they confessed and realized they were naked and afraid, God asked them, "Who told you that you were naked?" In other words, to whom are you listening? Don't underestimate the power of words. They can shape your way of thinking, which will eventually determine your direction. It is very important for each of us to stop and consider whose words we allow into our lives.

Ask yourself these questions: Where am I In the race of life? Who am I listening to?

Father, I am so thankful You are the great Shepherd. I know You hear every prayer and You see every tear I have shed. Jesus, You have clearly said Your sheep hear Your voice and they will follow You. Oh Father, please protect me from listening to anyone other than You. My eyes are on Jesus and I know it is His desire for me to be still and listen to His voice. I have so many voices that come in my mind throughout the day. I ask You to protect me from following any voice other than the voice of Jesus. May I go where You lead and may I be willing to shut out all the voices that aren't Yours. I love You, sweet Jesus, and I wait to hear from You. I'm Your child and I want only to follow You.

The Finish Line

*For I am already being poured out
as a drink offering, and the time
of my departure has come.*

The little boost of energy brought on by the cheers from the crowd didn't last very long. The only thing that stayed with me was one thought: I am tired, thirsty, and I want to quit. I needed something to push me to keep running, and I had no idea what that might be. The one thing I had was my pride, and that's never a good thing. Pride is so powerful that it can keep us from admitting our weakness to the point of self-destruction. It can make us willing to hurt the people we love before admitting our mistakes, much less changing our direction.

I had not seen my girls since we waved goodbye at the starting line. My mind filled with thoughts of my sweet girls and the rest of my family waiting for me when I crossed the finish line. I tried to cheer myself on with the occasional "Keep going!" and "Don't stop now!" I had to dig deep within myself to draw strength from what I now know is the power of God within me. I prayed, "God, I'm so thirsty. I need water. I can't do this anymore, nor do I want to. Please run this race for me." At that moment, I heard the loudest cheers I had heard throughout the entire race. Had I died? Was God applauding me into His presence? Was the race over? I was way too tired to be dead, and I could see that the road ahead of me—which was NOT golden, by the way— was covered with weary half marathon runners. Where were the cheers coming from, and the music, and all the clapping? Through my sweat and tears, I saw the banner ahead of me: **THE FINISH LINE.**

What?! Could it be true? Had I really finished the race? I began to pick up speed. Where in the world did that spark of energy come from? I had no idea, but oh how sweet the sounds of the cheering, the fun music, and the applause from the people. Everyone was cheering as I ran across the finish line! I can still feel the joy of finishing a race I never dreamt I could run. I stepped over the mat that would document my time. The race was over, and I ran every mile without training and without a drop of water. The thought of finishing was so sweet . . . until I actually crossed the finish line. Suddenly, everything around me started to spin. I grabbed a metal railing in front of me, trying to keep from falling down. To this day I vividly remember one particular lady and the look on her face as she watched me cross the finish line. I didn't know who she was and will probably never know her name, but the look on her face when I was spinning out of control is etched in my memory forever. She looked terrified.

I had run the race. I had finished the course, and now I had to face the consequences of my choices. I held on to the fence, trying to regain my composure, but it was useless. I struggled to find anything to hold on to until eventually I fell to the ground. I have no memory of anything else except waking to a man's voice saying, "No heartbeat! No blood pressure!" I had finished my race, but now I faced another struggle. My body had been pushed to its limit, and the consequences of the choices I made were in full force.

I had faith in myself that I could finish the race and have plenty of time left over to enjoy my family vacation. The dangerous decisions I made were not because I didn't have enough faith, or even because I had not trained. Yes, training and faith would have made a huge difference, but the real issue was the object of my faith.

My faith was set on my ability to run the race on my terms. The consequences I faced came from misplaced confidence in my own ability and unrealistic expectations of what was required of me. The lies I believed led to unwise choices, before and during the race. I found out the hard way that in order to run your race well, you can't go on feelings.

Every decision I made felt right and reasonable from my perspective. But I was wrong. What made me think I could run in a half marathon without any understanding of what was involved? I entered the race believing lies, and I finished reaping the consequences of them. Trust me, the race was a struggle from the beginning to the end. Pride is not a good running partner. This is true of my half marathon, and it's true of my spiritual race.

———

Over the course of my life, I have made many life-changing decisions with consequences that sent me into chaos and helplessness. God had to bring me to a place where I had nothing to hold on to but Him. When I first decided to follow Jesus, it was for His blessings and benefits. It was all about me. I thought I could live as I pleased, and if ever I got to a place where I needed God to intervene, I would call on Him and He would rescue me and make all things good.

How prideful I was, thinking the God and Creator of the heavens and earth was on standby, waiting to serve me whenever I summoned Him! I guess I had never taken 1 Corinthians 10:12 (NIV) to heart—"If you think you are standing firm, be careful that you don't fall!" Oh, and did I fall! After the half marathon, I fell flat on the ground, helpless and totally dependent on someone else to help me survive. If I was to live, God had to intervene. The first step in my spiritual race, and the last step in my half marathon, was total dependence on God.

True life began the moment I died to self and surrendered to the care of a loving Father.

I realize now that God had to humble me to get my attention. I have always been strong-willed, believing I can work things out so that I can get what I want in life. God loves me way too much to let me continue believing the lie that it's up to me to make things work out. God created me for Him, and He has a plan for my life—a perfect one.

One of the most powerful gifts God gives His children is the power to choose. I can understand why God allows us to choose to love and obey Him. I would never want anyone, including my family, to love me because they felt they were forced to. I want the people I love to love me out of their own free will.

I remember my mom saying to me, "Doris Ann, if you started hitting your head on a wall, you would keep going, even in pain, just to prove a point." Over the years, time has shown my mom to be correct. It's one thing when your mom has to prove she's in control, and it's another when God allows circumstances to show you He is in control. It's one thing to argue with your mom, but it's another (and completely unwise) thing to argue with God. I know from experience because I have done both! As I look back on my life, my greatest struggles have been with God. There have been times when I pleaded with Him to step in and take control of my circumstances, only to get mad when He didn't change them the way I wanted Him to. I spent many years trying to manipulate God to do what I wanted Him to do instead of surrendering to His will.

In the garden of Gethsemane, Jesus asked God to allow the cup He'd been given to pass from Him—the "cup" of the cross, that moment when God would forsake Him and He would die a physical death. And God said no! God did not answer Jesus' prayer the way He wanted it answered. Why? Because God wants His children to be able to come to Him, and the only way we can approach a holy God and have a relationship with Him is through the blood of Jesus. I can't bear to think what would have happened had God said "yes" to Jesus' prayer. I would have no hope of enjoying my heavenly Father. Life would have no meaning, and death would be final. Because Jesus humbled Himself and became man in order to die for all mankind, we are given access to our heavenly Father, forgiveness of sin, and life in Him.

I'm in awe of my God, who loves me when I am not lovable. He rescues me when I set out on my own to live life as I please. I have never walked or run down any path alone. In every area of my life and every difficulty I have faced, God has given me His strength, power, and peace. Shame and regret often keep us from experiencing the presence of God in our lives, but He never intended for us to run this race with shame. Jesus took our shame and placed it, along with all our sin, on the cross. Of course, we will be ashamed when we sin, and we should acknowledge our sin and ask for forgiveness. But after we repent, God forgives. Nothing can set you free like this truth: you are forgiven!

The life of the apostle Peter displays the power of God to forgive. Can you imagine the shame Peter must have felt when he denied even knowing Jesus, only hours after telling Jesus he would NEVER deny Him? Peter's pride led to his greatest regret. What remorse he must have felt when he turned to see Jesus looking at him! I often wonder if Peter could ever erase the look on Jesus' face from his memory. Jesus said He knew Peter was going to deny Him, and that he would be able to use the lessons he learned through it to strengthen his brothers in the faith (Luke 22:32). I think this is precisely why I've written this book. My prayer is that you don't make the same mistakes I have made.

I can truly say that, apart from my salvation, the best thing God did for me was allowing me to come to the end of myself. Surrendering your life to God's will is not easy. It's actually a little like dying. If we are to run the race God has set for us and live the life we long to experience, we must give up control and surrender to God's loving care. Let's face it, when it comes to life, we have no real control. God has the key to death and life, so there's not a person in this world who can add one day to his or her life.

God determines when our race is over and when our purpose has been fulfilled.

That's when He will take us home to be with Him. Until then, we are runners.

It might be helpful if we think about the circumstances in our lives—the ups and downs, the good and bad—as mile markers in a race. In other words, everything you have experienced in life is only a mile marker in the race God has asked you to run. The circumstances you face will be different from the circumstances I will face. We have our own races to run, and we make our own choices. I have had many "mile marker" events in my life. The half marathon is a small race compared to the race of being a wife, mom, sister, and friend, or the race to keep my focus on God when I'm tempted to fulfill my own desires. The apostle Paul compared the Christian life to struggling in a race.

To live a purposeful life with Jesus is hard, but to live a peaceful life without Jesus is impossible.

I finished the half marathon only to enter into another race, one directly influenced by the choices I made. It would have been so much easier to accept that I passed out at the finish line if I could blame Disney for it, but I couldn't. It was Disney's responsibility to map out the course, and it was up to me to train for that course. It was my choice not to train or drink water, not Disney's. In the same way, it's easier to blame God for the outcome of our lives rather than accept the consequences of our choices. Sure, there are parts of the race God asks us to run that are totally under His sovereignty, but for the most part, the determining factors in our lives consist of the choices we make and where we place our faith.

In Hebrews 12:2, the writer tells us to "[look] to Jesus, the founder and perfecter of our faith, who for the joy that was set before him endured the cross, despising the shame, and is seated at the right hand of the throne of God." Jesus came to die for us, and on the cross when He cried out, "It is finished!" His race, His purpose, and His will had been fulfilled. Jesus had finished what He came to do—rescue His children from sin and open the pathway for us to enter into the presence of God. His life was filled with sorrow and tragedy if we look at it through human eyes. Yet in the eyes of Jesus and through the eyes of faith, His life was made complete by being obedient to God.

There were many mile markers along Jesus' way, through temptation, rejection, betrayal, and even the unbelief of His close friends. But the cross was the final, most important mile marker in His human race, and what's surprising to me is that He finished with joy.

As a follower of Jesus, we will be asked to travel down similar paths. Don't be discouraged if you find your life headed in a direction you never dreamed you would have to travel. We all struggle with surrendering our will and embracing God's will for our lives. Personally, my greatest battles have been with God rather than with Satan. Most of the time I can discern the works of Satan, and when I do, I fight against his devious ways. But when I want God to do something either for me or for my family and He doesn't answer my prayers like I want, I fight against His will over mine. It's a struggle that doesn't seem to get any easier.

I had dreams of enjoying the spa, seeing the kids enjoy the Disney parks, and being with my family after the race, but I was robbed of experiencing those dreams. Actually, I robbed myself of them! Just like the letting go and grabbing hold principle we talked about earlier, sometimes the greatest thing we can do is die to our self-made dreams and take hold of the dreams God has for us. We have to come to a place of dying to ourselves to be alive in God. We must keep our eyes on Jesus and allow Him to lead us down His path with the mile markers God has prepared for us as we run with Him.

Remember how I said my pride and strong will made me determined that I would not be picked up by the sweepers? Yes, I technically ran the race by my own rules. But I was picked up at the finish line—not by sweepers but by ambulance—and taken to Celebration Hospital. I not only hurt myself, but I also hurt the ones who love me most. The tracker I wore on my shoe notified my family that I had finished the race. They began the search to find me, but to no avail. They tried to get into the first-aid tents next to the finish line, but the volunteers wouldn't allow it. Calling my phone wasn't helping because I didn't hear it; I was passed out! Each unanswered call added one more level of fear and worry.

Finally, after the paramedics had managed to stabilize me, they asked if they could answer my phone. The first voice my family heard was that of a stranger telling them I had passed out from exhaustion and dehydration and was heading to a hospital in an ambulance, with tubes and oxygen hooked up to my body. It was not my best moment! I was broken, and my pride was long gone. Now I needed a miracle; I needed God!

Sometimes coming to the end of ourselves isn't pretty, but it's necessary.

When He is all we have, we realize He is all we need and, in time, He is all we really want.

I hope that when I finish my race on earth I can say as Paul said, "I have fought the good fight, I have finished the race, I have kept the faith" (2 Timothy 4:7). Until then, I pray every day to continue to fight the good fight, keep the faith, and finish well, So how can we run our race without growing weary? According to Hebrews 12:1-2, we can do that by keeping our eyes on Jesus and running with Him, for Him, and because of Him.

It is difficult to continue our race when life is spinning out of control, but God has given us all we need to run well and to keep the faith. We can run through the streets of discouragement, resentment, bitterness, tragedy, and sorrow without losing our faith in God if we remember that the object of our faith is God, not ourselves. Sometimes people say, "If you just had faith . . .", but this is incomplete. We all have faith in something or someone. The danger is when we trust in something or someone more than we trust in our God. We must have faith in a loving and powerful God, not merely faith in faith. We enter into God's race by faith, we run by faith, and we finish well with faith. Faith is the key that opens the door to all God has for us. It is faith that allows us to put our confidence in a powerful and loving God who has our life in His sovereign control. It is faith in

God that allows us to "rest" in Him and not in ourselves. Faith IS the victory!

I found rest for my tired and weary body when I was placed on the stretcher and given the nourishment I needed to live again. Through Jesus, we are placed in God's family, and our faith in Him will provide all we need to survive this race called life.

Father, it's so hard to keep running when I get tired, weary, and discouraged. Just when I think I have finished one race, I find myself running again. The many mile markers I have passed tempt me to think You have walked away from me, but I know this isn't true. In the Bible, You have promised to never withhold what is best from Your children. Please remind me to dig deep within and draw upon the power of the Holy Spirit to empower me to keep running for Your glory. The prophet Isaiah reminds us that You are everlasting and You don't get tired. Thank You for this encouragement, Jesus. I love You.

Do You Know Your Name?

Therefore, if anyone is in Christ, he is a new creation. The old has passed away; behold, the new has come.

2 CORINTHIANS 5:17

tried to speak, but the words would not come out.

Thoughts were racing through my mind. *Who is this man? Why are they saying no heartbeat, no blood pressure? What has happened?* I guess the paramedic realized I had opened my eyes, because he asked, "Do you know your name?" I may not know a lot of things, but I certainly knew my name. I answered (correctly), and then he asked if I knew what I had done. I told him I had just finished a race. After I answered his questions, he completed the story by telling me I had collapsed at the finish line and was on my way to the hospital for treatment. I couldn't believe my ears. What was he talking about? I'm going to a hospital? To this day, I don't remember anything after becoming dizzy until I heard the paramedic talking about my vital signs. At the time, I didn't understand the seriousness of answering his two questions correctly.

Do you know your name? Do you know what you did? These two questions are foundational in the race of life. Our answer to one or both of these questions has the potential to give us hope, peace, encouragement, and strength to run our Christian race.

———————

When I look back on my life, I see how long I fought against shame and regret. I wish I knew then what I know now about who God is and who I am as His child. Sure, I know my name. But it took years, and I mean many of them, before I had even a glimpse of who I am as God's child. I believed so many lies about God and embraced lies that others threw at me with their words and actions. I know now that when my heart is broken over hurtful words spoken to me, I can examine and compare them against the truth of God's Word. I know I'm not the only woman who has lived most of her life believing lies about who she is and who God is. Many of us have grown so accustomed to false words and negative accusations that we are more comfortable believing them than we are believing the truth.

Before the half marathon, you would never have convinced me that I couldn't run the whole thing without water. In my mind, it just made sense not to drink water because I could have all the water I wanted after the race. I see this same mentality among many Christians. They believe they can live by their own rules and, when life gets difficult, they'll receive the life-giving water Jesus offers. But it doesn't work that way, trust me!

There comes a time in everyone's life when we are asked to surrender our wills to the sovereignty of God.

If we do not know the Jesus of Scripture, we will never enjoy our relationship with Him as His children. How will we surrender to a loving God if we don't know that He is love?

I know all too well how hard it is to surrender your will to a God you barely know. For most of my life, I knew I was going to heaven but I certainly wasn't having a good time on earth. Jesus was my Savior, not my life. When we come to the end of ourselves and reach out to the God who saved us, we find ourselves bowing before Him in repentance. True life begins when we embrace the truth that He is all we need in life. When I began to really learn who God is and the truth of His Son, I realized Jesus was sitting on His throne, cheering me on to enjoy victory as His child.

I first heard what it meant to live as a victorious child of God when we were attending First Baptist of Atlanta. One Sunday morning they introduced Bill and Annabel Gilliam as guest speakers for a weekend conference. Howard and I immediately signed up to go to the conference, unaware we were signing up for a life-changing event. That weekend, Bill and Annabel shared what it meant to walk/live as a child of God. I was never so happy to understand it was not up to me to live the victorious life, rather it was the Spirit of God living in me, empowering me to live the Christian life.

Paul writes in Romans 8:9-11, "You, however, are not in the flesh but in the Spirit, if in fact the Spirit of God dwells in you. Anyone who does not have the Spirit of Christ does not belong to him. But if Christ is in you, although the body is dead because of sin, the Spirit is life because of righteousness. If the Spirit of him who raised Jesus from the dead dwells in you, he who raised Christ Jesus from the dead will also give life to your mortal bodies through his Spirit who dwells in you." I sat in awe under the Gilliams' teaching, soaking up every truth they taught from the Bible. For the first time, I knew that God was giving me the truth I had prayed for and so desperately needed. If I were to live as a child of God, I needed to know and obey the truth that I have been set free from the bondage of trying to live the Christian life.

We were challenged to memorize Romans 6. I had never memorized one verse from the Bible, and certainly never an entire chapter. It was during this conference I knew God was asking me to renew my mind with this truth. If we are to walk in a manner worthy of our calling, we must embrace the truth that Jesus has released us from the power of sin. This does not mean we will never sin, just that the power of sin in us was destroyed by the blood of Jesus on the cross. As long as we are living in this world, we will encounter the presence of sin. Thank Jesus, the pull and power of sin has been destroyed and we no longer need to live in bondage!

In the book *Extraordinary Victory for Ordinary Christians*, Ron Dunn writes:

"A victorious life is not a superior brand of Christianity reserved for the elite of the elect. It is the normal life for every Christian. It isn't bestowed upon some because they are spiritual; it is given to all because they are saved." [1]

I struggled for so long to overcome all my weaknesses, when all the while God wanted me to see my weakness so He could be my strength. I was miserable and discouraged every time I had to ask God to forgive me "again" for doing the same things I knew were against His truth. Trying to live the Christian life in your own strength will leave you flat on your face, just like me at the finish line after the half marathon.

> *An athlete is not crowned unless he competes according to the rules. . . . Think over what I say, for the Lord will give you understanding in everything.*
> **2 TIMOTHY 2:5, 7**

It's hard to feel victorious when you are lying flat on your face, hopeless and defeated. That's why it is so important to know the truth that will set us free. Lies and sin will rob us of the life Jesus has died to offer us, but if we know the truth of who God is and embrace who we are as His children, we can live in freedom and joy. I cannot say this enough! I have experienced defeat and hopelessness in this life, but I've also known what it means to live a victorious Christian life. Let me tell you, nothing compares to living free when the world is tempting you to live in bondage. The Bible commands us to set ourselves apart from the world, and that is the key to living a victorious life. As much as I desired to live in freedom in my early Christian life, I discovered that to be free, I must be obedient. We are not to seek victory; we are to seek Jesus and obey Him. This leads to being able to walk in His victory.

> *No, in all these things we are more than conquerors through him who loved us.*
> **ROMANS 8:37**

When I first read this verse, I knew something was wrong. If the Bible says I'm a conqueror but I still lived in defeat for most of my life, what was I missing?

It's one thing to know the truth; it's another to believe the truth.

To live free and victorious I had to know the truth, believe the truth, and obey the truth. I had to stop believing what others said about me—all the lies I allowed to fill my mind and my heart—and replace them with the truth of who I am as God's child. Then I could embrace all the spiritual blessings I received the day I said yes to Jesus.

You may have a hard time believing what the Bible says about a child of God. It took me years to grasp the reality that I am victorious, righteous, and free. When I finally believed what God said about me, I began to live by truth, not by my feelings. When we embrace who we are in Him, we can live out who we are as new creations and our old patterns of sin will not overcome us. We will, of course, continue to deal with the presence of sin, but it's one thing to deal with the presence of sin and quite another to be entangled by it.

I felt so defeated most of my life, feeling I couldn't stop doing the very thing I did not want to do. This was a lie mixed with just a little truth. We cannot overcome sin in our own strength, but the Holy Spirit living in us empowers us to walk away from it.

If you are to run the race God has set for you, it's necessary to remove anything that is blocking you from keeping your eyes on Jesus. God went to great lengths to show us who He is by sending Jesus. And in light of who God is, we get a glimpse into who we are.

After finishing the half marathon, I had to face the reality that things did not turn out as I had planned. I had to answer those questions: Do you know your name? Do you know what you did? God asks those same questions. When I finally surrendered to God, He asked me to know who I am as His child—to understand that I am a new creation in Christ. In the race God sets for us, we must grasp who we are in Him, be honest before a holy God, and repent for the choices we have made that are keeping us from finishing strong. We have to fess up to what we've done wrong.

Whenever I get discouraged or feel alone and forgotten by God, I meditate on His names. There is power, hope, and strength in the name of the Lord!

Names of God

Yahweh-Yireh	God will provide (Genesis 22:13-14)
Yahweh Mekaddishkem	The Lord who sanctifies (Exodus 31:12-13)
Yahweh-Nissi	The Lord is my banner (Exodus 17:15-16)
Yahweh-Rapha	The Lord who heals (Exodus 15:25-27)
Yahweh-Rohi	The Lord is my Shepherd (Psalm 23)
Yahweh-Sabaoth	The Lord of hosts (1 Samuel 1:3)
Yahweh-Shalom	The Lord is peace (Numbers 6:22-27)
Yahweh-Shammah	The Lord is there (Ezekiel 48:35)
Yahweh-Tsidkenu	The Lord our righteousness (Jeremiah 23:5-6; 33:16)

Titles of God

1. Eternal Father (Isaiah 9:6; 1 John 1:1-30)
2. Faithful and True (Revelation 1:5; 3:14)
3. God (John 1:1, 14-18, Romans 9:5; Titus 2:13; Hebrews 1:8)
4. Head of the Church (Ephesians 5:23)
5. High Priest (Hebrews 3:1-2)
6. Holy One (Mark 1:24; Acts 2:27; 3:14; Psalm 16:10)
7. Hope (1 Timothy 1:1)
8. Image of the Invisible God (2 Corinthians 4:4; Colossians 1:15)
9. Jesus (Matthew 1:21)
10. Judge/Ruler (John 5:22-23; Acts 10:42)
11. King of Kings (Revelation 17:14)
12. Lamb of God (John 1:29, 36; 1 Peter 1:19; Revelation 5:6)
13. Living Water (John 4:10; 7:38)
14. Light of the World (John 8:12)
15. Lord of Lords (Revelation 19:16; 1 Timothy 6:15)
16. Messiah (John 1:41; 4:25)
17. Prince of Peace (Isaiah 9:6)
18. Redeemer (Job 19:25)
19. Shepherd (1 Peter 2:25)
20. The Way, the Truth, and the Life (John 14:6; Acts 9:2)

And here are some things God says about you. Did you know that THIS is who you are?

1. Able to do all things in Christ (Philippians 4:13)
2. Abounding in grace (2 Corinthians 9:8)
3. Accepted (Romans 15:7)
4. Appointed by God (John 15:16)
5. Beautiful (Isaiah 61:10)

6. Belong to God (John 17:9)
7. Bold and confident (Ephesians 2:18; 3:12)
8. Called (1 Corinthians 1:9)
9. Child of God (John 1:12)
10. Chosen (Colossians 3:12)
11. Christ is your life (Colossians 3:4)
12. Clothed with Christ (Galatians 3:27)
13. Confident He will never leave me (Hebrews 13:5-6)
14. Created in Christ for good works (Ephesians 2:10)
15. Free (Romans 8:2)
16. Made alive in Christ (Ephesians 2:5)
17. More than a Conqueror (Romans 8:37)
18. New Self (Ephesians 4:22-24)
19. No longer a slave to sin (Romans 6:6)
20. Protected (2 Thessalonians 3:3)

On the last day of the feast, the great day, Jesus stood up and cried out, "If anyone thirsts, let him come to me and drink. Whoever believes in me, as the Scripture has said, 'Out of his heart will flow rivers of living water.'"
JOHN 7:37-38

In order to have a close relationship with our God and Savior, we have to know His name and pray in His name. When Jesus was asked by His disciples to teach them to pray, He instructed them to pray in Jesus' name. Praying in Jesus' name does not mean we can manipulate Him to do what we want. Prayer isn't a magical formula; it's simply talking to God and seeking His will on earth as it is in heaven. God will always answer this prayer and give what is best for His children.

I have a resource I use in prayer called *Nuggets from Revealing the Treasures* by Sylvia Gunter. In this pamphlet, Gunter outlines who God is and who we are in Him. We don't truly know God or ourselves until these truths become profoundly real in the core of our being. A divine exchange took place when we made a new covenant with our heavenly Father through confession of our faith in Jesus. He gave us His character, His nature, and His essence, which are represented by His names. All that He is became ours.

It's truly mind-blowing for me to think that I am united with Christ. I do not live; Christ lives in me. If you really want to get your heart racing, meditate on this:

And we know that the Son of God has come and has given us understanding, so that we may know him who is true; and we are in him who is true, in his Son Jesus Christ. He is the true God and eternal life.
1 JOHN 5:20

May I be as bold with you as the paramedics were with me? Do you know your name as a child of God? Do you know what you have done?

Victorious life is yours the moment you surrender who you were before Christ and embrace who you are now in Christ.

Father, how great and marvelous are Your ways! I want to be still before You to seek Your face and not Your hand. When I make my requests known to You, may I be reminded of all You have already given me as Your child. I thank You for the Holy Spirit living within me. May I draw upon the Holy Spirit to empower me to live life in victory and in freedom. Oh great God, I'm in awe when I remember You are in me! May I never waste another day looking back to what I have done, but look forward because of all You have done for me. Please receive my praise and worship as I bow before You. I love You, Jesus!

CHAPTER NINE

Free to Run

*For freedom Christ has set us free;
stand firm therefore, and do not
submit again to a yoke of slavery.*

GALATIANS 5:1, NIV

Howard heard the voice of a stranger answer my phone. A paramedic told him I was in an ambulance on the way to the hospital after collapsing at the finish line. My sweet husband had just buried his mom a few weeks before, and now he was facing the possibility of losing his wife. I cry even now thinking about how much pain and anxiety I caused my family.

In all the years we have vacationed at Disney, Howard has rented a car every time—except for this one. When he made the travel arrangements, he declined a rental car since we were staying at the Grand Floridian and we could ride the monorail in and out of the park. I can only imagine the chaos in the hotel lobby as my family rushed in, crying and pleading for a 12-person taxi to Celebration Hospital. The name sounds so joyful, but I can assure you, no one was celebrating at this hospital. When I arrived, the faces of the nurses told me all I needed to know—I was in danger.

I found out later that two other runners in the same race had died that day. On the day I left, the nurses told me that they didn't think I would leave the hospital alive. I was so dehydrated that my body was trying to attack my organs. I am so grateful to God for giving me the gift of another day. Not only did He give me a second chance at life, but all of my organs are fine. This is nothing short of a miracle!

I can't express how I felt when I saw my family at the hospital. I could see they had been crying, and the concern on each of their faces opened wide the regret and shame I felt for all the stupid decisions I had made. It's one thing to reap the consequences of them and hurt yourself, but it's another when you see your choices bringing pain to the people you love.

This year my son, Scott, ran his first marathon at Disney, and our whole family went to cheer him on. When we came to the finish line to see Scott cross, I felt sick to my stomach. As I stood there waiting, everything came back to me. I could see the lady's face when I tried to hold on to the rail. I often wonder if she was the one who called the paramedics to help me. I wonder if God keeps that image clear in my mind as a reminder for me to encourage and equip women to run their race and finish strong.

I remained in the hospital for our entire stay in Orlando. I never saw the kids enjoy the rides in the park. I never stepped foot into the beautiful spa at the hotel. The only time I saw my children was when they rotated time with me at the hospital. The choices I made before and during the race did not determine the final destination. Disney determined the path and I determined the outcome. The consequences of my choices were set in motion when I decided to run by my own rules. The same is true in your Christian race. God determines the destination and the rules, and we can choose to obey God's rule or live with the outcome of our choices.

From the beginning when God created man, He made the choice to give you and me a choice. If we choose to destroy our lives, He will allow us to. I can't blame God for the consequence of my own decisions. I found out the hard way that every choice I made set into motion the consequences of that choice.

> *To reap the consequences of our choices does not nullify God's forgiveness.*

Forgiveness has nothing to do with reaping consequences. While I will reap the consequences of each sinful choice I make, God will still forgive every single one. I guess this is why God's grace is so amazing and His forgiveness is unfathomable.

I was thrilled, to say the least, when the nurse came in my room and said, "You have been released." I felt like a new woman, and I had a much greater appreciation for running! I never want to live under condemnation and I don't want to ever forget what God has rescued me from. I need to remind myself daily that even though I finished the half marathon, I didn't finish strong. God used the race to bring me to a place of surrender, giving Him all that I had. I had been given the freedom of choice, and I suffered the consequences of my choices—chaos, pain, and heartache.

We often think we're in control when we make a choice. Yes, we have the power to choose, but once we use this power, the choice takes control. God used the half marathon to show me how to keep moving forward when life doesn't turn out the way I hope. My heart still gets sad over being robbed of enjoying the rest and relaxation of our family vacation. I allowed my pride and ignorant choices to rob me of the joy of experiencing all that I had been looking forward to. I can't go back and undo what I did, but I can learn from my mistakes and move forward.

If you think of life as a race, it's easy to see how the things that happen to you along the way can either destroy you or inspire you. If you believe in the sovereignty of God as I do, you can face life's circumstances as part of God's perfect and loving plan for your life. God orchestrates every detail in all circumstances and uses them for His purpose. Yes, our choices will make a difference in our direction. But God takes every choice, every decision, and He uses each one as an opportunity to teach us His ways and lead us down the path He has paved for us.

Consider each of the disciples Jesus called to follow Him. They each had a different purpose that fit perfectly in Jesus' plan. Matthew was a Jewish tax collector who became one of Jesus' disciples. His gospel connects the Old Testament to the New Testament because of the emphasis on fulfillment of prophecy. The apostle John was called the one Jesus loved. He wrote the book of Revelation, giving us hope and proclaiming the victorious reign of King Jesus. Peter knew persecution firsthand. Beaten and jailed many times, his very life was threatened. Yet he is known for his denial of Jesus. Peter's message is a powerful one because he knew what it meant to suffer as a follower of Jesus. All of these men and many more finished their race strong.

Jesus is the greatest example of all for how to run our own race. Jesus made it perfectly clear why He came: to glorify the Father and to seek and save the lost (Luke 19:10). Just before His darkest days, Jesus prayed in Gethsemane and asked God to remove the cup He had been handed, a grueling death on a cross and being forsaken by His loving Father. But His love for you and me kept Him on the cross until He could proclaim, "It is finished!" His life and His death were mile markers in the purpose of His coming. Jesus was released from death to give us life, and His power was magnified when He walked out of the tomb. Because of Jesus and all the spiritual blessings He offers to His children, we can face our lives with the confidence that we don't run alone!

As you look over the life-changing events in your life, can you see the hand of God leading and encouraging you to keep running? The writer of Hebrews encourages us to do just that:

> *Therefore, since we are surrounded by so great a cloud of witnesses, let us also lay aside every weight, and sin which clings so closely, and let us run with endurance the race that is set before us, looking to Jesus, the founder and perfecter of our faith, who for the joy that was set before him endured the cross, despising the shame, and is seated at the right hand of the throne of God.*
> **HEBREWS 12:1-2**

There is nothing you will face in your life that Jesus has not already faced, including suffering. Your Savior offers you living water to satisfy every need you have. He is sitting at the right hand of God, cheering you on as you run the race He has asked you to run. He knows you by name and allows you to enter into the presence of a Holy God through His blood and by His name.

Jesus has released you from the power of sin so that you can run faithfully for His glory.

These are the benefits of living life as a follower of Jesus.

When I walked out of the hospital, I was released to live again. I was overjoyed to walk out of the hospital with my loving family by my side. When I received Jesus as my Savior, I was given a new life—His life. I get the privilege of walking each day with Jesus. I would never again want to experience what I experienced in my half marathon, but the lessons I've learned from it have encouraged me to run strong in the race God has asked me to run.

I pray that you, too, are encouraged as you to take these lessons to heart and keep running for God's glory. Maybe your life has been surrounded with every imaginable obstacle known to man, and you feel like you're too tired to try again. Please do not hear me say that it's easy to pick yourself up and start running, especially when you have no desire or strength to even walk. I know how easy it is to give up, and how exhausting it is to strive to live above your circumstances, to live free from the expectations of others, and to find the strength to move forward when you have been knocked down by circumstances that were totally out of your control.

If that is you, take comfort from God's words through the prophet Isaiah:

"Have you not known? Have you not heard? The LORD is the everlasting God, the Creator of

the ends of the earth. He does not faint or grow weary; His understanding is unsearchable. He gives power to the faint, and to him who has no might he increases strength . . . They shall mount up with wings like eagles; they shall run and not be weary; they shall walk and not faint"
ISAIAH 40:28-29, 31

It's not easy to follow the path Jesus has asked us to travel, but it is possible. Not only that, we can run with confidence and faith. How? By depending on the Spirit of God who lives within. His power will allow us to run without growing tired, discouraged, or weary.

The determining factor between the success and failure of my half marathon was as simple as drinking water. Even if I had trained, the outcome would have been the same without the necessary water. The same is true in the race God has asked me to run; I have to drink living water. Jesus told the woman at the well that if she knew who He was, she would ask Him and He would have given her living water that satisfies her desires (John 4:10). In the same way, Jesus stood and proclaimed to everyone on the last day of a feast he was at, "If anyone thirsts, let him come to me and drink. Whoever believes in me, as the Scripture has said, 'Out of his heart will flow rivers of living water.'" (John 7:37-38). How do we sustain ourselves in the race of life? We must stop trying to fulfill our own desires and allow Jesus to satisfy our thirsty souls. Only Jesus can satisfy our natural and spiritual longings with His grace, love, and mercy. As a matter of fact, it's Jesus who will keep us running with purpose and freedom.

In 1968, John Stephen Akhwari represented Tanzania in the summer Olympics in Mexico City. He had finished first in the African Marathon Championship previously and was a world-class runner for most of the 1960s and 1970s. Due to the high altitude in Mexico City, Akhwari experienced muscle cramping in the Olympic race. He had not trained at such an altitude back in his country. At the 19 kilometer point during the 42-km race, there was a scuffle for position between some of the runners, and he was hit. He fell, hitting his shoulder on the pavement and badly wounding and dislocating his knee. However, he continued running, finishing last among the 57 competitors who completed the race (75 had started). As he crossed the finish line, cheers came from the small crowd in the arena. When interviewed later and asked why he continued to run, he said, "My country did not send me 5,000 miles to start the race; they sent me 5,000 miles to finish the race."

I have tried to picture the scene when John Stephen Akhwari entered the arena as one of the last runners of the race. Only a few spectators saw this Olympic runner, all beaten up with barely enough strength to put one foot in front of the other, as he crossed the finish line. Seeing the finish line and hearing the small applause, I wonder if his emotions took over to give him the extra strength needed to run across the line.

We are told the small crowd cheered and the media immediately ran to record history being made. I would love to have a conversation with him and ask if he ever doubted he would finish. I'm pretty confident he did not expect the applause and the lifelong attention he has received from never giving up. Maybe he did not consider his race a success, but had he finished with the other 57, I do not believe we would be as inspired today as we are from his strong will to keep running. He was awarded a National Hero Medal of Honor in 1983. The 1968 Olympics was John Stephen Akhwari's greatest platform to inspire others to never give up! What others might call his greatest defeat became his greatest victory.

How about you? Is life getting you down? Are you discouraged and losing all hope that your current circumstances will change for the better? Are the consequences of your choices stealing from you the will to keep living? Do you struggle with shame? Does it feel too late to ask God to forgive you and give you a fresh start? It's never too late to start again! We cannot give up hope. As children of God, we all have a reason to be hopeful. We have a God who is cheering us on to fight the fight and to keep the faith.

Our faith isn't dependent upon changing circumstances, but it's in a God who never changes.

God will love us through our successes and failures. Jesus left heaven to offer us everything we need to run the race He has asked us to run. The mistakes and failures of others do not determine the outcome of your race. Just like John Stephen Akhwari and the life of every child of God who has run their race, we must keep running until we cross the finish line, finishing strong.

Father, I have tried to be strong when in reality, I need to be weak. In my weakness, You are made strong, and it is Your power I need to keep running the race You have asked me to run. Until I see You face-to-face, I will trust You to empower me to run the race You have mapped out for me. I love You, sweet Jesus!

Conclusion

But, as it is written, "What no eye has seen, nor ear heard, nor the heart of man imagined, what God has preparred for those who love him."

1 CORINTHIANS 2:9

As I lay helpless in the ambulance, I remember asking the paramedics, "Did I get my medal?!" I had IVs and oxygen tubes on my body and a frantic family on the phone, and my one concern was whether or not I got my ridiculous fake gold medal at the finish line. They told me I had, in fact, gotten my medal. Somehow it was a small comfort in that moment. It's funny that I don't remember getting it, but I do remember wanting it!

Jesus told His disciples that He must go away so that He could prepare a place for them. That place is for us, too, and we will cross the finish line of our race the moment Jesus calls us home. I have a feeling that when I enter into the presence of God after my race on earth comes to an end, I will want to receive the reward for running. But even more than this, I long to place each treasure at the feet of Jesus as a "thank you" for all the riches and blessings He has given me as His child!

The Bible promises that in heaven there will be no more tears, no more trials, no more pain, and no more unfulfilled desires. That is a beautiful promise, but as I think about that first moment in heaven, as much as I long to see my parents and my dear friends I've had to say goodbye to, nothing will compare to the joy of finally seeing the face of Jesus! The thought of hearing Him say, "Welcome home!" and seeing Him reach for me with His nail-scarred hands makes all the pain, uncertainty, and struggle worth it. To hear "Well done, good and faithful child," is a great reward, but greater still will be living with God for eternity.

In his letter to the church at Corinth, the apostle Paul says that eyes haven't seen, ears haven't heard, and minds haven't conceived of all that God has prepared for those who love him (see 1 Corinthians 2:9). And in Hebrews, we are encouraged to keep our eyes on Jesus, the "the founder and perfecter of our faith, who for the joy that was set before him endured the cross, despising the shame, and is seated at the right hand of the throne of God. Consider him who endured from sinners such hostility against himself, so that you may not grow weary or fainthearted." (Hebrews 12:2-3)

Jesus faced opposition, pain, struggles, rejection, and sin without growing weary, and He has given the Holy Spirit to empower us to face each of these and keep running. The message our sweet Savior is speaking to us is clear in another of Paul's letters to the Corinthians:

> *But we have this treasure in jars of clay, to show that the surpassing power belongs to God and not to us. We are afflicted in every way, but not crushed; perplexed, but not driven to despair; persecuted, but not forsaken; struck down, but not destroyed; always carrying in the body the death of Jesus, so that the life of Jesus may also be manifested in our bodies. For we who live are always being given over to death for Jesus' sake, so that the life of Jesus also may be manifested in our mortal flesh. So death is at work in us, but life in you. Since we have the same spirit of faith according to what has been written, "I believed, and so I spoke," we also believe, and so we also speak, knowing that he who raised the Lord Jesus*

will raise us also with Jesus and bring us with you into his presence. For it is all for your sake, so that as grace extends to more and more people it may increase thanksgiving, to the glory of God. So we do not lose heart. Though our outer self is wasting away, our inner self is being renewed day by day. For this light momentary affliction is preparing for us an eternal weight of glory beyond all comparison, as we look not to the things that are seen but to the things that are unseen. For the things that are seen are transient, but the things that are unseen are eternal.

2 CORINTHIANS 4:7-18

As we run the race God has set for us, we can find hope, peace, and joy knowing that whatever road we must travel, pain we must endure, tribulation we might encounter, or battles we may fight, they are not meaningless.

We can face every trial knowing that when we finish our final race, God will be standing at the finish line applauding us because we fought the good fight and kept the faith.

The writer of Hebrews reminds us Jesus left heaven and came to earth. Jesus did not leave heaven and come to earth for us to give up. Jesus came to encourage us to never give up, and in His power, we are more than a conqueror!

I have read the last chapter in the Bible and it says that when heaven and earth pass away, God will make a new heaven and earth. Finally, we will enjoy the life God intended us to live from the beginning of creation. Until our life is over and we enter into the presence of God, we will face one challenging race after another. The exciting news is that at the final finish line, in Jesus we win! I encourage you to meditate on the words of John when the Spirit of God gave him a glimpse into our future:

> *"I, Jesus, have sent my angel to give you this testimony for the churches. I am the Root and the Offspring of David, and the bright Morning Star. The Spirit and the bride say, 'Come!' And let the one who hears say, 'Come!' Let the one who is thirsty come; and let the one who wishes take the free gift of the water of life."*
> **REVELATION 22:16-17, NIV**

Therefore, we must keep running with Him, for Him, and because of Him. I would love to share with you an illustration that brought me peace after my mom finished her race and entered into the presence of God. It's a wonderful description of heaven from Max Lucado's book, *The Applause of Heaven*. I pray this illustration will encourage you to keep running your race until you cross the finish line.

"I'll be home soon. My plane is nearing San Antonio. I can feel the nose of the jet dipping downward. I can see the flight attendants getting ready. Denalyn is somewhere in the parking lot, parking the car and hustling the girls toward the terminal.

I'll be home soon. The plane will land. I'll walk down that ramp and hear my name and see their faces. I'll be home soon.

You'll be home soon, too. You may not have noticed it, but you are closer to home than ever before. Each moment is a step taken. Each breach is a page turned. Each day is a mile marked, a mountain climbed. You are closer to home than you've ever been.

Before you know it, your appointed arrival time will come, you'll descend the ramp and enter the City.

You'll see faces that are waiting for you. You'll hear your name spoken by those who love you. And, maybe, just maybe—in the back, behind the crowds—the One who would rather die than live without you will remove His pierced hands from His heavenly robe and . . . applaud!"[2]

There's never a day I do not long to hear my mom's voice and to share the daily events of my life with my mom and dad. I know they are waiting for me, and only God knows when I will run my last race and enter into His presence. When my mom and dad went to be with Jesus, I tried to find every verse in the Bible about heaven. I wanted to know what my parents were experiencing in their new home. Over the years of getting to know Jesus more, I now long to see His face and worship Him with a heart of praise and thanksgiving before I see my other loved ones. When I first decided to accept the call of Jesus, I wanted heaven more than I wanted Jesus. Over the past several years, I now want Jesus more than I want heaven. I have discovered that wherever Jesus is, there is heaven!

One final thought before we part: when you enter into the presence of God, it will be Jesus who presents you as

His gift to your heavenly Father. Isn't that a wonderful thought? I am Jesus' gift to God, and so are you!

> *Now to him who is able to keep you from stumbling and to present you blameless before the presence of his glory with great joy, to the only God, our Savior, through Jesus Christ our Lord, be glory, majesty, dominion, and authority, before all time and now and forever. Amen.*
>
> **JUDE 1:24-25**

Father, I have no other words than to say thank You for giving me life in Jesus—who is heaven's Olympic runner! He ran His race and He finished strong. He is now seated at Your right hand, cheering His children to run their race. It's been a long journey, but now I know the life worth living is a life lived in Jesus. Now, I long to hear the applause of God and every child of God who has finished their race and is now with Jesus. I long to see Jesus stand, extending His nail-scarred hand to me as He welcomes me home. What a race worth running! I love You, Jesus!